Writing from the Fringe

Born at Narrogin in Western Australia in 1938, Mudrooroo Narogin left Perth for Melbourne in the 1950s. He studied at night while working in the Motor Registration Office and the State Library. He wrote *Wild Cat Falling*, and then travelled in Asia and India, particularly in Thailand where he continued to study Buddhism. He later spent several years in India, three of them as a monk.

Returning to Melbourne in 1976 (via Perth and the US), Mudrooroo Narogin worked at the Aboriginal Research Centre at Monash University, studied at Melbourne University and taught at Koorie College. He then moved back to Perth to tutor in Aboriginal Literature at Murdoch University and spent a year writing full time on a Fellowship from the Western Australian Department of Arts Development Fund. In 1988 he lectured in Black Australian Literature at the University of Queensland. He is now working on his fifth novel, a film script adaption from his novel, *Dr Wooreddy*, and an anthology of Aboriginal writing.

By the same author:

Novels by Colin Johnson
Wildcat Falling
Long Live Sandawara
Doctor Wooreddy's Prescription for Enduring the Ending of the World

Novels by Mudrooroo Narogin
Doin Wildcat: A Novel Koori Script as constructed by Mudrooroo Narogin

Poetry by Colin Johnson
The Song Circle of Jacky and Selected Poems
Dalwurra: The Black Bittern

Writing from the Fringe

A Study of Modern Aboriginal Literature

Mudrooroo Narogin

HYLAND HOUSE

First published in 1990 by
Hyland House Publishing Pty Limited
10 Hyland Street
South Yarra
Melbourne,
Victoria 3141

© Mudrooroo Narogin 1990

Publication assisted by the Australia Council, the
Australian Government's arts funding and advisory body.

National Library of Australia
Cataloguing-in-publication data:

Narogin, Mudrooroo, 1938–
 Writing from the fringe: a study of modern
 Aboriginal literature.

 Bibliography.
 Includes index.
 ISBN 0 947062 55 6.

 [1]. Australian literature—Aboriginal authors
 —History and criticism. 2. Australian
 literature—20th century—History and
 criticism. I. Title.

A820′.9′89915

Typeset by Solo Typesetting, South Australia
Printed by The Book Printer, Victoria

Contents

Note on the cover illustration

SONG OF LIFE by Terry Dhurritjini Yumbulul

A long time ago in the beginning of time, the goannas were called by the Creator to assemble near a billabong. Here they were given the songs and dances and stories of creation, then the Creator sent them to populate the land.

Many years passed and the animals populated the land, then 'man' came and the animals had the job of teaching 'man' the laws of the land so they went back to the billabong and here, as the goannas danced, 'man' was taught the laws of life. To remember this day 'man' still imitates the dance of the goannas as it happened a long time ago.

This is a Dhuwa painting belonging to the artist's mother's tribe, painted by Terry Dhurritjini Yumbulul of the Warramiri tribe of Wessell and English Company Islands, NT.

(Courtesy Emerald Hill Gallery, Melbourne)

To all the Aboriginal writers who made this book possible. To all my old students at Murdoch University and the University of Queensland who debated many of the points raised. I hope they learnt as much as I did. To Patrick White for his support in 1988.

Ellen sat picking at her fringe of leaves. The corroboree was over, except the embers, the ashes, and the continued exchange of hoarsened voices.
Patrick White, *A Fringe of Leaves*

Acknowledgements

The author wishes to thank the following for permission to quote from their works: Mark Bin Bakar for 'Fly Away Pidgin', transcribed from the audio-cassette *Kimberley Legend* (n.d.), sung by Lucy Cox; Ted Egan for 'Tjandamara' transcribed from the audio-cassette *Ted Egan Presents the Kimberley* (n.d.); Lionel Fogarty and Penguin Books for 'Free Our Dreams' from *Yoogum Yoogum* (1982); Oodgeroo of the tribe Noonuccal, custodian of the land Minjerribah, and Jacaranda Wiley Ltd for 'My Love' and 'Cookalingee' from *My People* (1970).

Introducing the Fringe

I am seeking the truth of my countries
where the ancestors lived in the past.
I am far away from my country
and my family's living in a different way.
In my memories I hear the song of my tribes . . .

Ruthie Marrwulpul

ABORIGINAL LITERATURE BEGINS AS A CRY FROM THE HEART directed at the whiteman. It is a cry for justice and for a better deal, a cry for understanding and an asking to be understood. In some ways it is different from other national literatures which are directed towards a national readership and only after that to other nations. Black writers, such as Kevin Gilbert and Oodgeroo Noonuccal have a White Australian readership firmly in mind when they write and it is their aim to get across to as many people as possible the Aboriginal predicament in Australia. A predicament which has resulted in many Aborigines becoming strangers in their own land, so alienated that sometimes they seem to have lost the will to survive. Invasion, occupation and dispossession have resulted in the coming into being of a people without visible means of support, a *lumpenproletariat* objectified in these lines from my *Song Circle of Jacky* (1986, p. 31):

> The shuffling drunk the street derides,
> God staggers by in drunken rage.

Both white and black writers have written of the predicament and this has resulted in a strong literature which is evergrowing. But it may be said that over the last decades conditions have improved and with this improvement Abor-

1

iginal literature has began to turn towards cultural and self-introspection. Guilt and blame are not enough for the continuation of a literature, and so histories from an Aboriginal viewpoint are being constructed. Life stories (often in collaboration), novels, short stories and poems are devoting their words to the Aboriginal existential being in what is now said to be a multicultural Australia.

These topics are not new, though they are becoming of increasing concern to Aboriginal writers. From the strong beginnings of Aboriginal literature in the sixties and seventies, Kevin Gilbert, a major writer of the fringe states in *Living Black* (1984, p. 3), that the existential predicament of the modern Aborigine resides in 'a rape of the soul'. In his works, he consciously analyses the decay of Aboriginal society which has occurred and is occurring all across Australia, seeing it as the result of a historical process rather than as a reality to be endured as Archie Weller appears to do in some of his stories, such as 'Pension Day' in his book *Going Home* (1986, pp. 68–73).

These two writers are critical of the degradation often found within Aboriginal communities. They do not romanticise this culture of poverty in which drunkenness plays too great a part, in which pensioners are robbed of their pensions by youngsters, in which cruel revenge is taken, in which parents gamble the day away while their children stumble around brain-damaged from sniffing petrol. The coarseness of life is painful to witness—in fact it may seem that entire communities are deliberately attempting to wipe themselves out; but Aboriginal writers refuse to see this as an inherent trait, or as a social Darwinism based on an evolution which stresses that only the strong shall survive and that when a people is confronted by a different race equipped with strange and terrifying things, then everything is lost and that people unable to adapt become extinct.

Aboriginal writers developing away from the urge to establish a connection between the races of Australia have turned their attention towards understanding the dilemma of their people and their communities. It would be easy to blame the watjela or gubba for all the ills of Aboriginal communities, but they refuse to take this negative trail though they are fully cognisant of what happens to a people which has suffered a rape of the soul with continuing effects to the present. Perhaps this picture written is too white and it would be if Aboriginal writers only concentrated on the evils which bedevil Aboriginal society, but they also write of the bright things, the human warmth, the spontaneity and humour with which life and its problems are faced. Still, in introducing a study on Aboriginal literature, before we proceed to examine the texts and their presentation, the existential condition of Aborigines and their historicity must be taken into account. Aboriginal literature does not exist in an aesthetic vacuum, but within the context of Aboriginal affairs. It must be seen holistically within a cultural, historical and social context. To try and approach Aboriginal writers and their literature as things existing apart from their communities would be a falsity. Not only this, but contemporary Aboriginal communities are the end result of 200 years of white history, and this past must never be forgotten.

Aboriginal writers may be labelled 'committed' writers. They all are deeply concerned with the problems of their communities even to the extent that community is stressed at the expense of the individual. In writing about these problems, they become aware of similar problems facing minorities in Australia and other countries of the world and give their support to those communities fighting for a place under the sun, free from the domination of national majorities. Still, they acknowledge that their primary goals are to understand their own communities, the basis of their literature, and from there to create a literature which will not only be of use to the community, but will help to spread a knowledge about the Aborigines of Australia and their unique culture. These are their aims. Aims often shared by some white academic and creative writers.

To have an understanding of this literature coming from the different communities—the Nangas, Nyoongahs, Djamadjis, Murris, Kooris, Yolngus and the other regional groups making up the unity of people placed under the white term, *Aboriginal*—there first must be a general schema of history which may be fleshed out from the works of the writers and storytellers.

I will divide Aboriginal history into a number of periods and it is these periods which not only go towards forming the style of the writers of the fringe, but also supply the contents of their works

THE DIVISIONS OF ABORIGINAL HISTORY

1. *From the Beginning to 1788:*
   The Dreaming; Prehistory; Before The Coming of the Europeans.
2. *The Time of the Invasion(s):*
   For the first time, the Aboriginal peoples of Australia are confronted with another people who come not to visit, but to conquer. Around the areas of conquest they go down under the onslaught. Aboriginal culture is placed under threat, and begins to change and adapt new ways of communication.
3. *The Utter Conquering of the Aboriginal Peoples:*
   A typical oppressive colonial-type regime is established in Australia. Many of the old ways of communication are destroyed, or drastically changed.
4. *The Colonial Period:*
   At first there is outright oppression which gives way to paternalism, then a policy of assimilation. The remnants of the peoples are to be forced into the mainstream of European civilisation. Opposed to this are a number of Europeans such as anthropologists who seek ways of preserving Aboriginal cultures.
5. *The Period of Self-Determination:*
   This dates from the time of the Whitlam Government in the late 1960s and is still continuing, though with a strong tincture of assimilation. It is a time when the Aboriginal communities are penetrating official Australian history and life as a people with definite aims and objectives. It is the time of the rise of an identifiable Aboriginal literature, distinct from collections of myths, and with a certain ideology of *Aboriginality*.

Aboriginal being and history until now, the last period, has been dominated by *Anglo-Celts*. *The Time of the Dreaming*, is called *prehistory* and a whole theoretical structure has been erected with little recourse to the Aboriginal communities. As with possibly all conservative communities, the past was the basis for all explanation of the present and future. This way of placing time and things in a continuum is called *mythology* by Europeans and is contrasted with the scientific way of thinking which seeks to explain the past from the present. Scientists and scholars prefer to work backwards from what is now to what was and tend to ignore any accounts found in the mythology of the Aboriginal communities, though this mythology is the *oral records* of the communities. Different scholars argue different things from the evidence they collect and often their accounts and theories seem more fantastic than the myths they seek to replace. Their investigations wander over and under the land. They measure and chart data from which they postulate things about the Aboriginal people: whether they are one or many, whether they have remained in the Stone Age or not.

Theories are fashioned and discarded like European fashions, and as there is a history of fashion so there is a history of theories. This is called anthropology. A genealogy of much speculation is the origin of the Aboriginal people. We have been said at different points of the genealogy to have been here from the beginning; to once have been part of the ancient population of Gondwanaland; to have floated here, either deliberately, or accidentally after walking across Indonesia when the seas froze during the last Ice Age and the islands became a single landmass except for one wide stretch of water. This last theory at the moment is the one generally accepted. It is popular because it has political implications. The Aboriginal peoples may be seen as the first immigrants and *thus* just like the other peoples in Australia though it is admitted that we arrived on the continent some tens of thousands of years before anyone else. This means politically that we were the original possessors of Australia. This genealogy of theory may be contrasted with Aboriginal history as contained in the oral records. There it is stated that some peoples have been here from the very beginning of humanity. Later arrivers, such as the Wawilak sisters and their brothers, landed to find the *country inhabited.*

It must be admitted that the beginnings of Aboriginal occupation of Australia are lost in the mists of time. It is difficult, if not impossible, to place a definite date on when human beings arrived. Often, forty or fifty thousand years is stated, but these dates have been arrived at by dating archeological sites such as Keilor and Lake Mungo in Eastern Australia. Scientifically, all that they say is that at that time people camped, or buried their dead there.

Few if any peoples can date their origins with any certainty. Mythology only tells of the events happening when they were created, or when they arrived at a certain country. If dates are given, they often are found to have been added long afterwards. In Australia, many myths dealing with the origins of the different Aboriginal communities have either been lost, or incorrectly recorded. This means that much of the oral literature of the Aboriginal people is no longer available for examination and that it is impossible to deconstruct records dealing with each and every community. Some extant accounts describe events which happened thousands of years ago. These may provide dates when people were in a certain area. Thus there is an account which describes the eruption of volcanoes around Mount Gambier in South Australia which happened some six thousand years ago.

Oral literature is important in that it describes Aboriginal life in Australia before the invasion, though I must modify this to say that the formal oral literature as preserved in religious cults may be considered to have suffered less change and thus is more reliable for reconstituting pre-invasion Aboriginal lifestyles. This oral literature often detailing the early wanderings of the creative ancestors, or ancestral beings, in lines of long songs has received some study. A theory has it that the routes of these beings are early migratory trails along which the different communities travelled to spread all over the continent; but this is uncertain. The portions which are still treasured show that Australia was never a trackless wilderness. If all these records had been collected, a detailed road map might have been constructed. As it is, the surviving fragments are important to Aborigines and others as a classical literature. In future it may serve as an aesthetic basis for the written literature. They are as important to the Aborigines as the *Iliad* is to Europeans.

The Time of the Dreaming, the time of the great epics, lasted for thousands of years. The first British settlement at Port Jackson marks an end of this period, and the beginning of a steady decline of Aboriginal culture and literature. Remains of that traditional culture and literature may be found scattered throughout various books of ethnology and in the minds of numbers of men and women. Some scholars, for example the anthropologist T. G. H. Strehlow in his *Songs of Central Australia* (1971), collected, translated and explained parts of this literature.

There are collections of stories and legends which preserve examples of pre-invasion literature, though often these are heavily Europeanised. The uniqueness of Aboriginal communication and the aesthetic use of language is lost in the translation. It is only recently that scholars are beginning to be concerned with *narrative discourse*, the way in which the story is told and structured, but in many areas it is too late to collect authentic structures of Aboriginal narrative discourse in the original language. The languages have been replaced with an English of varying degrees of standardisation.

The Time of the Invasion(s) began when Europeans visited the shores of Australia. Dutch, French and British established initial aggressive relations which were not propitious for the future. William Dampier the first Englishman to land on the western coast of the continent met Aboriginal resistance which drove him back to his ship. In his journal, he made a number of assertions which for the next centuries, with a short interlude for the concept of the noble savage, were to be held by most European invaders. In his words, the people differed but little from brutes.

It may be said that such statements are neither made lightly, nor innocently. Colonisation had to be justified by a Christian people which prided itself on a superior morality and culture. One way of doing this was by seeing a people in possession of a wanted land as being uncivilised, savages or even animals. British colonial expansion was not a blind immoral course of action, but a deliberate policy with an ever shifting ideology of justification behind it. Thus the British sailing to establish a settlement at Port Jackson rehearsed their ideology. They speculated on the place of the Aborigines in creation and arrived at a consensus that they occupied the bottom-most rung on the ladder of humanity, along with the various primitive peoples of Africa and the Americas. This, in their opinion, was justification for the invasion of lands already inhabited.

The different Aboriginal communities also had their own ideology when meeting with Europeans. There are oral accounts of Aboriginal people meeting Europeans for the first time, and some writers have put down accounts of when they first saw Europeans. One of these, the Walmajarri writer, Peter Skipper, in his book, *The Pushman* (n.d.) has given a short account of when he came in from the desert and of how he reacted to the Gadiya and their strange animals and objects. An overriding emotion was fear, but there was an ideological framework into which Europeans could be incorporated. The pale skinned strangers were accepted as ghosts of the deceased returning. Modern Aboriginal writers in English, using oral and written sources, have reconstructed accounts of the initial contact.

At Port Jackson, after the first contact the Aborigines appear to have avoided the English invaders, perhaps in the hopes that they would return to their ships and sail away. But the settlement was permanent and an active Aboriginal resistance under Pemulwuy began. Smallpox arrived with the invaders. It became an epidemic and effectively ended Aboriginal resistance. Koori writers, such as Bobby Merritt, in his play, *The Cake Man* (1978) have portrayed the effects of the invasion. Eric Willmot in his historical novel, *Pemulwuy, the Rainbow Warrior* (1987) has detailed Aboriginal resistance around Port Jackson. Other writers, including Jack Davis, James Miller and myself have dealt with this period in plays, histories and novels.

Throughout Australia, as the weakened and demoralised

tribes went down or fell back before the guns of the colonists, a more compassionate invader came to soothe the pillows of a dying race. These were the Christian missionaries who although they saw Aboriginal culture as intrinsically pagan and thus evil, did bring with them a policy of education which in effect helped to foster the first Aboriginal writings in English. One of the first Aboriginal writers, David Uniapon, was the product of a mission school. Some missionaries, for example the Germans C. G. Teichelmann and C. W. Schurmann in South Australia even used the native language, but eventually English became the language of instruction. The missionaries laboured to soften the coarse pioneering spirit of the first settlers, who often considered the Aborigines vermin to be destroyed. They accepted the Aborigines as human beings and educated them and eventually Christianised them so that today there is a strong current of Christianity running through much of Aboriginal writing.

As soon as Aboriginal resistance was crushed, there began a period of complete colonial subjugation. The peoples were herded into mission or government stations. Those outside on the vast cattle runs and farms which had been carved from their homelands were exploited for their labour value. In fact punitive laws were passed to prevent them from leaving these stations. They in effect became slaves, working for rations of tobacco, sugar and tea. While the men worked in the fields, the women worked as domestics in the homesteads of masters who weren't averse to the soft feel of 'black velvet'. Aborigines were outside the white law, or incarcerated under special Aboriginal laws which prevented them from any assertion of rights. In fact they were declared 'wards of the state' and had no rights. Any resistance was put down by the police, or settlers. The result of this oppression is what is often accepted as the public face of the Aborigine: shiftless, dirty drunken natives fighting and carrying on without hope for a future of grace and dignity.

There was slight mixing between the two races except during the course of work and for sexual intercourse between whitemen and black women. This led to the rise of a *mestizo* class, the coloured or half-caste, people of colour who served as intermediaries between the two races. They might even find a place in the white township and be allowed to drink in the hotel. But the separation of races was instituted from the beginning of the invasion and has continued to this day. These times have been described in works by Aboriginal writers and white writers. The biography of Jack Davis is one example.

Separation and domination continues in many rural areas of Australia to this day and has resulted in the deaths of Aboriginal people. Jack Davis' play, *Barungin (Smell the Wind)* (1989) is about Aboriginal deaths at the hands of police. The death of one young man, John Pat— allegedly kicked to death by the police in the streets of Roebourne, Western Australia in 1983—has led to any number of poems. Aboriginal literature suffered a loss when the promising poet, Robert Walker, was brutally killed in Fremantle Prison, Western Australia in 1984.

In Australia a policy of separation, and economic conditions, forced many Aborigines into living on the fringes of white towns. This has been the subject of a play, *Coodah* (1986), by Richard Walley. A gap is shown to exist between white and black and this is bridged by the *mestizo*, the do-gooder and the missionary, though these latter intermediaries were constantly under attack for seeking to educate the native. A. O. Neville, the Commissioner of Native Affairs in Western Australia, and a character in two of Jack Davis' plays, *Kullark* and *No Sugar*, was no friend of the missionary or of education for the Aborigines. He described the Nyoongah people thus:

> 'A nameless, unclassified outcast race, increasing in numbers but decreasing in vitality and stamina, and largely unemployable . . . They have very little in the way of education, but some of them have just enough to enable them to become defiant and unrestrained.'

Richard Walley in *Coodah* and Jack Davis in his realist drama, *No Sugar*, depicts these days under this commissioner, and the conditions and rules under which the Nyoongah people had to live. Robert Bropho in his work, *Fringedweller* (1980) describes the conditions on the so-called native reserves and the problems faced in the search for decent living standards. These authors do not accept the explanation that Aborigines are not used to proper houses, and must do with sub-standard housing, tin sheds for which they must appear grateful. Instead they demand adequate shelter, a sense of human dignity and fair play towards their community.

The existential being of the Aborigine in Australia has been seen by some white writers to be akin to that of a child, but it is Aboriginal writers who seek to explain this result as stemming from a paternalist attitude which forced the Aborigine into the attitude of a child asking for help from a benign white person. Under the gaze of 'the other', the Aborigine became as a child. Unable to help himself, he sat waiting for the kind adult to offer succour, and this was often forthcoming. But for all his assumed being of child, he was not a child, but an adult, and his act of continuing bad faith led him into a self-hatred. An adult gazed into a mirror and saw not the face of a child smiling back, but the scowling face of an adult. This instead of leading to action, often led only to confusion and a passivity which was strengthened through alcohol. Drunk and stumbling bleary-eyed through life, he indeed could pretend to be a child. This state of abjection is portrayed in the play, *The Cake Man* by the character Sweet William living a childlike existence on a reserve.

In *Because a Whiteman'll Never Do It* (1973), Kevin Gilbert shows how wounding such paternalism is. Because Aborigines are treated as children, children of nature, not quite human, but quite charming on occasion and able to perform simple tasks, disease, crime and poverty may be put down to their childlike nature. Thus they need to be looked after on the missions; the paternal station owner may take care of the rest using them as slave labour, while the fringe dwellers, the half-castes unable to help themselves, must be bred into the European population and assume adult status as the child blood is diluted.

This attitude of *paternalism* lasted officially until 1937 when representatives of all the state governments came together to discuss the Aboriginal problem. The problem was what to do with them. Victoria had almost solved the problem by genocide; New South Wales reported much the same success with only a miserable remnant living on reserves or mission stations and a growing body of people of Aboriginal descent living in extreme poverty on the fringes of country towns; Western Australia and Queensland still had large populations of Aborigines living cowed in missions and stations kept under control by stringent laws; while the Northern Territory had a huge problem in that the Aboriginal population still outnumbered the white and if steps weren't taken they might eventually take over the state.

Different states formulated different policies to deal with the problem. Western Australia declared that it was going to merge the native race into its white community. Queensland decided that it was going to keep the Aboriginal population under paternal care and control on special reserves. This was until recently their policy though, like an angry father, the authorities could expel troublesome children from their homes, or even place them in special centres of detention such as Palm Island. The Northern Territory's policy was to keep the majority of the Aboriginal population firmly under control in missions, except for those *coloureds* who might be bred into the European population.

It was declared outright that the reason behind this policy was fear: fear of a people of Aboriginal descent eventually breeding into an underprivileged, angry militant majority. A result of this policy has been the separation of so-called coloureds from Blacks. In Western Australia the policy of assimilation was used as a tool of separation. A split developed between the assimilated and the unassimilated which is still seen today. Most Aboriginal writers writing in English are a direct result of such divide and control policies. Assimilation did give them a limited education, though it must be admitted that the incarceration of the most militant Aborigines in the prisons also helped the rise of Aboriginal writing in English. Prison for many Aborigines has been their college. But the experience has often led to a literature of anger and frustation rather than to a literature of Aboriginality based on traditional forms.

The Aboriginal writers who arose in the sixties were the products of assimilation revolting against assimilation. Assimilation was seen as the policy of division, of seeking to alienate individual Aborigines from their communities and pushing them into European society. These individuals, it was hoped, would be completely estranged from their families and become like Europeans. Children were forcibly removed from their parents and placed in institutions. These became the only homes these people ever knew and it is a sadness of the policy that today some Aboriginal people knowing no other childhood look back with fondness on these institutions. In Western Australia numbers of Aborigines became completely institutionalised, and made the trip down the Canning River on which most of these institutions were located to the port of Fremantle and the prison there. They could exist nowhere else but in an institution and the outer world was a frightening place to be deadened by grog until the inevitable happened and they found themselves safely inside again.

The policy of assimilation attempted to submerge a dark minority, the remnants of the victims of a brutal colonisation, in Anglo-Celtic life and culture without questioning the right to do so. A first step was to make all Aborigines wards of the state without any rights of citizenship. They were trainee citizens who had to earn their right to be white. But in tandem with assimilation went a racism which effectively broke the policy. Even when granted citizenship rights, Aborigines still found themselves discriminated against, still found that they were not accepted by the white majority. They were caught in a no-man's-land between Black and White. To the Whites they were considered black and to the Blacks they were considered quislings or 'Jackies'. It was from these contradictions that there arose the struggles for dignity in the mid-sixties when a benign government came to power, and when there were enough

Aborigines formally or informally trained to lead the struggle. Aboriginal writers such as Oodgeroo Noonuccal and Kevin Gilbert were at the forefront of the struggle, and have been there ever since.

At this time the political struggles for justice, land rights and self-management were developed. The struggle still continues and it is difficult to see any result or lasting achievement coming from it. In fact with increased education and job opportunities there is an impetus towards a merging into the majority culture, identified here as Anglo-Celtic. Thus the stage of active struggle for an independent identity may be passing. Assimilation, although discredited, still operates through government education and employment policies. New writers such as Sally Morgan and Glenyse Ward do not see themselves as part of an active ongoing movement, but as individuals either searching for their roots or seeking equal opportunity in a multicultural Australia. It might even be said that Aboriginal affairs is entering a stage of post-activism in that any separate goals are being replaced for those of equal opportunity in the wider Australian community.

This was clearly seen in 1988 when two hundred years of white rule was celebrated. Some Aboriginal writers saw the year as an opportunity to forge links between the Aboriginal minority and the white majority. The poster for the Aboriginal day celebrations (NAIDOC) bore the slogan 'Come and Share Our Culture'. Any separatist sentiments were downplayed and there was a return to a call for understanding such as we find in the poems of Oodgeroo Noonuccal dating from the first rise of Aboriginal literature in the early sixties. Thus there might seem to be a movement away from a literature being used as a weapon to raise the consciousness of Aboriginal people and to articulate their concerns.

Activist literature has moved to a literature of understanding. A literature not committed to educating individuals as to their place in Aboriginal society, but one committed to explaining Aboriginal individuals to a predominantly white readership. It is significant that in 1988 creative writing was replaced in importance by the life story. A form of literature akin to biography and auto-biography, but having its roots in the methods of the American anthropologist Oscar Lewis. This is a heavily edited literature often written and revised in conjunction with a European. Its message is one of understanding and tolerance, which may be a good thing in regard to an Aboriginal place in a multicultural Australia, but it is a literature dealing only with the past. It is not concerned with the future aims and aspirations of the Aboriginal people. The closing words of Glenyse Ward's, *Wandering Girl* (1988) reveals the accommodation found in this literature:

> We will be making sure that our
> Kids will be given every opportunity
> In their lives to get a good education,
> So that they can take their places
> In today's society as Lawyers or Doctors,
> Or etc. — and be equal in the one human
> Race!

1

Writers of the Fringe

I N *ABORIGINAL WRITING TODAY* (1985 P. 53), DENIS WALKER, an activist and the son of Oodgeroo Noonuccal, states:

> Aboriginal writers have a responsibility here, a very important responsibility, to take that message, not only to white people but to Aboriginal people as well, so that we can foster within our own communities a very important concept. That concept is that if we are going to survive, we are going to have to do it as a community, we are going to have to do it as a nation and not as individuals.

He clearly sees that Aboriginal literature is the expression of an indigenous minority not only living on the fringes of the majority community, but as a separate nation of people which until the last two decades was completely under the heel of the oppressor. This meant many things to Aboriginal people: for example they did not do things, but had things done to or for them, and any urge towards protest or expression by them was fiercely attacked as being the work of others, i.e. radical whites. This is still the case among what may be termed the rightwing Whites of Australian politics, such as Geoff McDonald who in his book, *Red Over Black* (1984) tries to prove that all Aboriginal protest is a communist plot.

In a dusty file in the Mitchell Library in Sydney lie the

papers of William Thomas, an early settler of Tasmania. Included among his papers is a handwritten journal produced by Tasmanian Aborigines in their exile under the direction of the superintendent of their station, G. A. Robinson. This is an important journal in that it contains the first writings by Aboriginal people. The writers were Walter George Arthur, Peter and David Bruny. The journal was titled *The Flinders Island (Weekly) Chronicle,* and its object was 'to promote Christianity, civilisation and learning amongst the Aboriginal inhabitants, be a brief but accurate register of events of the colony moral and religious'. In 1837 it appeared every Saturday, was priced twopence and profits were distributed among the writers. The superintendent of the station intended the paper to be read as much by Europeans as Aborigines for most of the latter never learnt to read.

The writers for this journal appear to have been typical mission boys, those who were Christianised enough to enjoy the privilege of living next to the Europeans and sharing in their lifestyle. The still pagan majority were left as fringe dwellers around the mission and were to be coerced towards Christianity and civilisation. In this coercion, the mission boys as members of their race, had a large part to play. The boys who wrote for the paper were also sent around to the other Aborigines to keep them in line and to guide them towards civilised Christian values.

The Flinders Island (Weekly) Chronicle is the forerunner of much later Aboriginal literature in that it was controlled, but for all that it makes interesting reading. We learn how the Aborigines felt during island exile when their numbers were lessening under the impact of homesickness and they were held in a settled life in a camp set up on an inhospitable island. It was a vehicle of Aboriginal protest and a cry of help directed at the white people. We read this protest and cry in the 17th of November issue of the journal:

The brig *Tamar* arrived this morning at Green Island. I cannot tell perhaps we might hear it by and by. When the ship boat comes to the settlement we will hear the news from Hobarton. Let us hope that it will be good news and that something may be done for us poor people they are dying away the bible says some or all shall be saved but I am much afraid none of us will be alive by and by and then as nothing but sick men amongst us why don't the black fellows pray to the King to get us away from this place.

This newspaper is the first written expression of Aborigines in Australia, and although it must be admitted that G. A. Robinson had a hand in the production—for in the prospectus it is stated 'Proof sheets are to be submitted to the commandant for correction before publishing . . .'—it is rash to dismiss it as being completely composed by him. In fact it is similar to much later Aboriginal literature in that it is edited by a white person.

The next piece of early Aboriginal writing is a petition written to the Aboriginal Protection Board in Victoria. This too is protesting at conditions, and is historically important in that it was the subject of a police inquiry, for it was believed that the Kooris did not have the skills necessary to produce such a work. The Aboriginal station— or mission, or settlement—Coranderrk, was a centre of resistance in Victoria. As it was close to Melbourne, the Aborigines could demonstrate in the city and write letters to sympathetic newspapers. The Aboriginal Protection Board refused to believe that Aborigines were capable of using the pen, and in 1882 employed a detective to prove that the petitions and letters were forged by whites. A Detective Mahony went to the Coranderrk Station incognito only to discover that the letters and petitions were indeed written by a Koori, Thomas Dunolly, and were genuine expressions of the feelings of his people.

White people find it difficult to credit Aborigines with the production of a written literature, and as white editors and others have been involved in producing many Aboriginal texts, this attitude is perhaps justified. Not only this, but up until recently, all Aboriginal texts were prefaced with introductions acknowledging the work as Aboriginal. These prefaces and introductions have a part in any study of Aboriginal literature, and we are entitled to ask what exactly do they do besides authenticating the book?

I see them as not only introducing the writer to the reading public, but also inviting the reader to accept Aboriginal literary productions in certain ways. In effect, they are signals which often apologise for the Aboriginality of the texts which sets them apart from the grand tradition of European literature, that is there is a certain way texts should be written, and on occasion Aboriginal texts do not adhere to this. Whatever we may think of these prefaces, it is difficult not to accept their underlying message that Aboriginal people are not part of the majority culture and that they are fringe dwellers on the outskirts of the Metropolitan literary tradition of Europe.

Aboriginal literature is often considered to be a literature of protest, and thus outside the European literary tradition with its emphasis on universality. The fringe position of 'protest' literature is seen in an article in *English in Africa* (1, 1980): 'Evaluating Protest Fiction' by Gareth Cornwall. He begins his paper with a quotation from *Why I Value Literature*, by Richard Hoggart. This quotation is important in that it sets out the Metropolitan position on literature, which may be seen to be in direct opposition to the aims of Aboriginal literature. The quotation is:

> I value literature because of the way—the peculiar way—in which it explores, recreates and seeks for the meanings in human experience; because it explores the diversity, complexity and strangeness of that experience (of individual men or groups of men in relation to the natural world); because it re-creates the texture of that experience; and because it pursues its explorations with a disinterested passion (not wooing nor apologizing nor bullying).

Gareth Cornwall regards this statement as non-contentious; but the very fact of emphasising a 'disinterested passion' would make Aboriginal writers shudder and dismiss the rest of the paper as 'gammon'. Men and women are passionate beings engaged in the world, and writers are part of that passionate collective being engaged in the world.

The Aboriginal writer, Oodgeroo Noonuccal has a different view of the writer and her life and works bear it out. Here, I give in full her opening speech for the Second Aboriginal Writers' Conference held in Melbourne, Victoria in November 1983:

Dear Fellow Delegates
Today we have come together to work towards implementing a programme of action in the interest of Aboriginal writers and Aboriginal people. We can be proud of our past efforts. We, as writers, know only too well, how powerful is the pen, how much mightier than the sword. In our short history of progress, since the invasion, (and let us not forget), with little or no thanks to the invaders and their records, our history according to them began on the 27th May, 1967, when we the Aboriginal people, forced a referendum upon the peoples of Australia. So it is assumed by white Australians that we stagnated politically and economically throughout our long history in this our own country. What the mainstream of non-Aboriginal people in this country refuse to acknowledge, is that we were and are as a race, politically and economically sound, and have been so, since our Dreamtime. It is time we put the record straight. Through research, we, the writers must find our own historians and as you know Colin Johnson already leads that field together with Kevin Gilbert and others who have done much. Children's literature is very much to the fore, also. Our poets are well-known and much read. Our playwrights are not only seen but are also heard. But in spite of what we have achieved, there is still much to be done. FIRSTLY. We must at all times be critical of all fields of Aboriginal affairs. We are responsible to the people to ensure that the National Aboriginal Conference (NAC), for instance, is worthy of our praise and support. I personally am of the opinion that the NAC was and still is a toothless tiger—it is time they were armed with strong teeth, capable of biting. Their attitude to the Aboriginal Treaty (The Makarrata) is a glaring example as to what tame cats they are. I believe the Makarrata is the step in the right direction for our people. My personal thanks go to our friends who have worked long and

hard to provide us with a worthwhile document to base our fight on for the future.

SECONDLY. We must also write about black public servants. I feel sure you will agree with me that the Aboriginal input in this field leaves much to be desired.

THIRDLY. Our education field is a mess. The reason being of course that the present education scene in Australia does little or nothing to improve the lot of even the non-Aboriginal students. If we must be educated, then we need our own Aboriginal teachers and our own schools where, if desirable, non-Aboriginal students may attend.

FOURTHLY. The legal services. Let us clean up the bulldust that exists in this very important field. Let us ensure that before long we have our own Aboriginal lawyers, barristers, yes, and even our own judges.

FIFTHLY. Medical services. This field, in my opinion, is the only field that is truly dedicated to Aboriginal political action. I commend what they have done so far. May they continue to agitate in the interests of our people—but when will we see our doctors and nurses emerge in this field?

Regarding such fields as the Aboriginal Development Commission (ADC)—much has been done here, but little input has occurred in the urban and city fields. What must be understood by ADC is that allocating houses to rent or buy is a non-event if the tenants of such houses are unemployed. The ADC must therefore go further and create job opportunities in conjunction with Aboriginal Housing. Private Enterprise is *not* a dirty word. Aborigines have always worked within the Tribal situation of togetherness so private enterprise through co-operatives should not be impossible.

In the DAA and ADC it is very hard to find Aborigines working at the policy-making level.

In the Aboriginal Arts Board only one Aborigine works at staff level. As one of the newly-appointed Directors of the Aboriginal Arts Board, I give my word that that situation will change. These are the things that we must write about. Let the writers lead the field in advising, criticising and scrutinising the ideas and ideals in the interest of all our people . . .

Before I officially open this Second National Aboriginal Writers' Conference, I would like to sum up my speech by reading you the BLACK COMMANDMENTS:

1. THOU SHALL GATHER THY SCATTERED PEOPLE TOGETHER.
2. THOU SHALL WORK FOR BLACK LIBERATION.
3. THOU SHALL RESIST ASSIMILATION WITH ALL THY MIGHT.
4. THOU SHALL NOT BECOME A BLACK LIBERAL IN A WHITE SOCIETY.
5. THOU SHALL NOT UPHOLD THE WHITE LIES IN A BLACK SOCIETY.
6. THOU SHALL TAKE BACK THE LAND STOLEN FROM THY FOREFATHERS.
7. THOU SHALL MEET WHITE VIOLENCE WITH BLACK VIOLENCE.
8. THOU SHALL REMOVE THYSELF FROM A SICK, WHITE SOCIETY.
9. THOU SHALL FIND PEACE AND HAPPINESS IN A STABLE, BLACK SOCIETY.
10. THOU SHALL THINK BLACK AND ACT BLACK.
11. THOU SHALL BE BLACK ALL THE REST OF THY DAYS.

Oodgeroo Noonuccal espouses for the Aboriginal writer a far different role than that espoused by conventional Anglo-Celtic writers. If we need search for comparisons we might look towards African literature which appears to be concerned with people rather than self, though we should always keep well within mind that there are significant differences between African and Aboriginal literatures, and what we are seeking is not an identification with, but an elucidation of those problems we have in common. I again emphasise that I am not writing about a national majority, but an indigenous minority encapsulated and at the same time living on the fringes of an intruder majority. The Australian Aboriginal experience equates more with such minorities imprisoned within so-called national boundaries throughout the world, rather than with any type of racial majority be it white or black.

Traditional Aboriginal societies were highly functional, and as the modern idealistic writer of Aboriginality identifies with this tradition, he or she does not espouse an art for art's sake as a governing aesthetic concept. Indeed all aspects of traditional Aboriginal culture were part of a holistic concept of society and to demand an antisocial place for an artist was undreamt of. Art was a social act and as can be read in Oodgeroo Noonuccal's manifesto, this has carried through to the modern writer.

Aboriginal artists are socially committed, and therefore have this commitment firmly in mind when they write. It is part of the tradition of Aboriginal culture to perceive the artist not as an isolated individual, alienated from his or her society and interested in only extending the bounds of his or her own private vision, but as a value creator and integrator. Scratch an Aborigine and beneath his or her apparent modern skin, or the persona he or she shows to the white world, you will find the old hunter or gatherer. The political activist, Bruce McGuinness, on reading Archie Weller's novel, *The Day of the Dog* has this to say about it in his paper published in *Aboriginal Writing Today* (1985, p. 47):

> I believe that Archie Weller has been able to give us an insight into the very distinct cultural forms that are kept, and which grow from one particular insight that I suppose the Aboriginal people on the reserves have when they move to the cities—they are forced by moving into the cities to come into closer proximity with other cultures. They are forced to exist there. They become hunters and gatherers within that city, within the new urban life, and to be hunters and gatherers there they have to change their weapons. The spear and the boomerang and the woomera are no longer acceptable weapons within the city area. They must change their mode of weaponry that they used to survive with.

The Aboriginal writer is a Janus-type figure with one face turned to the past and the other to the future while existing in a postmodern, multicultural Australia in which he or she must fight for cultural space. This creates a tension which on occasion may lead to an outright condemnation of all European writings on Aborigines as being *gammon*, and not worth the paper they are written on. It is this stress which creates the passion with which Aborigines view the world and their literature. They believe that a literature to be worthwhile must have social value not only to the individual, but to the community as well.

Aboriginal writers are not content with only writing about a past separate from their present being. The past is there only to explain the present and postulate ideals for the future. Still, the past is of the utmost importance in that it is there that true Aboriginality resides. This may lead to an idyllic picture of a past Aboriginal civilisation. For example, the first part of the video mini-series, *Women of the Sun*, scripted by Hyllus Maris, presents an idealised picture of natural harmony and contentment. Other writers such as Kevin Gilbert write about the recent past to expose the hidden underside of Australian history in which Aborigines were butchered, buggared and beaten wherever they made a stand, or attempted to retreat. This past is still with us. Survivors are still living, and I think that the awfulness of man's inhumanity to man should be dealt with until it becomes accepted as part of official Australian history. It is only then that Australia may free itself of its blood debt and the festering wounds of discontent.

It is no use declaring, as some Aborigines do declare, that the past is over and should be forgotten, when that past is only of two hundred years duration. It is far too early for the Aboriginal people to put aside that past and the effects of that past. Aboriginal people must come to realise that many of their problems are based on a past which still lives within them. If this is not acknowledged, then the self-destructive and community-destructive acts which continue to occur will be seen as only resulting from unemployment, bad housing, or ill-health, and once these are removed everything will be fine.

Bruce McGuinness, in his paper from which I have already quoted, calls for a *community control* of literary production and distribution. Anglo-Celtic writers recoil from this. They see in it an overall tyrannical censorship which they have had to fight in their own culture. Censorship means different things to different people. In calling for *community control*, Bruce McGuinness believes that he is striking against a censorship which is often covert, rather than overt, that because the Aboriginal writer must make his or her works amenable in style (and often in content) to the standards of publishers who have their eyes on the marketplace, this censors out Aboriginality of style and content. A problem here is that the Aboriginal population is too small with little economic clout, and so books for and by Aboriginal writers are goods of little profit, or if they are to be profitable must be written to conform to the dictates of the marketplace. Thus possibly our best poet, Lionel Fogarty, is forced to go outside the established publishers to have his works printed. His voice is a voice fighting to be heard, and at present it is heard mainly by Aborigines and by those who take Aboriginal literature courses.

Lionel Fogarty is the strongest poet of Aboriginality yet published, though in editions which are not readily available. His poetry makes no compromises towards the marketplace and is layered and textured into shapes and meanings which are difficult for European readers to understand. It is in direct contrast to other Aboriginal poets, such as Kevin Gilbert, who utilise traditional European verse forms for their message. Their meaning is as direct as a bullet and a person of the Anglo-Celtic literary tradition might find them most distressing, but they are impossible to reject, as was Lionel Fogarty's first book of verse (*Kargun*) by a critic writing in the periodical, *Aboriginal History* (6, 2, p. 115):

> In fact the most impressive aspect of this book *Kargun* — in terms of skill — is the talented graphic illustrations by Aboriginal artist Johnny Cummins of Cairns.

In contrast to Aboriginal writing, Aboriginal music is a field of Aboriginal expression which owing to the establishment of such associations as The Central Australian Aboriginal Media Association (CAAMA) and outlets on Aboriginal radio programs, remains under the control of Aborigines. CAAMA has begun recording Aboriginal musicians and so has Abmusic in Western Australia. Aboriginality is to the fore in that some Aboriginal languages provide the vehicle of communication and there is little aping of American or British speech patterns in the song texts in English. Many are in the genre termed country and western but a rhythm akin to Jamaican reggae is employed by some bands such as Coloured Stone and Modern Tribe. This type of rhythm appears to fit Aboriginal English speech patterns. Native instruments such as the didgeridoo and clapsticks have been successfully employed by some of the bands. No Fixed Address, originally from South Australia, was the most successful and the forerunner of a new generation of bands, which moved away from country and western. Constantly on the road, hence the name No Fixed Address they have recorded two albums which are still constantly played on Aboriginal radio programs, though they were released some years ago.

As Aboriginal music originates from the Dreamtime, it may be thought that drama is a development based on indigenous traditional forms. This is not so. Aboriginal drama is akin to other modern forms of Aboriginal expression, in that message either determines the form or uses a form ready to hand. Most of the dramas so far produced have a strong realist slant with intrusions of what may be termed *Aboriginal reality* or *Aboriginality*.

Jack Davis is the most successful of the Aboriginal playwrights. His productions are constantly moving towards pure Aboriginality in that they have from the beginning explored the limitations of the conventional European theatre, but as yet there is no escape from realism into a Theatre of Aboriginality utilising the Aboriginal environment of ceremony to recreate a symbolic drama drawing heavily on traditional structures. To observe this we must go to the Aboriginal Dance Theatre under the direction of the Afro American, Carole Johnson.

Jack Davis is a poet as well as a playwright. His verses are carefully worked rhythmic structures directed at a European readership. His philosophy of writing has been expressed in the late lamented Aboriginal periodical, *Identity*, where his concern for grammar may have bent his commitment to Aboriginality in form and content, though he has modified his stand since those times.

Aboriginal periodicals such as *Identity* have always concerned themselves with Aboriginal affairs as well as literature. I doubt that it would be possible for any Aboriginal periodical to deny commitment to the Aboriginal people and concentrate purely on art for art's sake. Many of the first generation of Aboriginal writers were published in *Identity*. The novelist, Archie Weller, had his first stories published therein. *Identity* collapsed some years ago and as yet no national magazine has arisen to take its place. The Aboriginal Writers Oral Literature and Dramatists Association (AWOLDA) has plans to begin a new magazine, but as yet these plans have not borne fruit.

The Aboriginal novel is a fragile flower still in the process of blooming. A problem is length. Only extracts can be published in Aboriginal periodicals and the cost of having a novel privately printed is prohibitive. It is relatively easy to run off a few dozen copies of a slim volume of poems on the photocopier of an Aboriginal organisation, but extremely difficult to do several hundred pages this way. The only recourse is to apply to recognised and hopefully sympathetic publishing houses, but this means that the novel is threatened by the editing processes of the publisher. In 1988, Magabala Books under the control of the Aboriginal community in Broome, Western Australia was established. It published the successful life story, *Wandering Girl* by Glenyse Ward. Perhaps in future it will expand its operations to publish books Australia-wide, though there still remains the problem of distribution.

The novel is a tool of reflection and it may be said that at this time the Aboriginal novel is in a state of reflection. Only my fictional work *Doin Wildcat* utilises Aboriginal speech patterns throughout. A recent novel, *Pemulwuy, The Rainbow Warrior* (1987), by Eric Willmot, though it is important in its subject matter in calling attention to the Aboriginal resistance fighter, Pemulwuy, breaks no new ground and is a conventional historical novel with even the Aboriginal characters speaking in proper English tones. Except for *Doin Wildcat*. there is no sign that the Aboriginal novel will break radically from European-derived models.

In *The Wretched of the Earth* (1973), in his section on

national culture, the African theorist, Frantz Fanon postu-lated three levels in the development of a literature of a colonised people. The first level, or phase, is when the native intellectual gives proof that the culture of the occupying power has been assimilated, and his or her writings then correspond point by point with those of their opposite numbers in the mother country. Inspiration is European and these works may be linked with definite trends in Europe. The native writes to show the colonists that he or she has mastered the genre. As an example, I may give my novel *Wildcat Falling* (1965) with its emphasis on the outsider and laced with quotations from Samuel Beckett. I add here that a minority finds it difficult to escape the influences of the encircling majority, and that the Aborigines in Australia are under an intense and constant cultural barrage which may in future utterly destroy their culture except for some fossilised traditional remnants. I believe that it is up to the writer to resist this barrage and strive to create works based on Aboriginality.

Fanon's second phase is when the native is not part of his or her people, has only exterior relations with them, and is content to recall their lives. In effect he or she is alienated from them and seeks elsewhere for his or her well being. The writer may produce books inclined towards pleasing the masters rather than accusing them. The aping of the Europeans increases, and masterpieces hailed in Europe may be produced and be completely ignored at home. This phase gives way to a third phase, the fighting phase in which there is an upsurge in literary production, with many people who never thought of creating beginning to create. Aboriginal literature is in this phase. There are people writing today, who once would never have thought of writing. 'What me write a book — you must be kidding!' But although, a few of these books are trying to avoid the encircling majority and not be dark imitations of the metro-politan culture, the majority may be placed in one genre or another.

I feel that it is away from the printing houses of the established publishers that an originality of Aboriginal writing is to be found. There is an increasing number of

Aborigines writing who do not go through the processes of being published. Their works are produced in small editions on equipment in the Aboriginal settlements and are for local consumption. They are usually in Kriol or the local language, and because of their limited appeal can escape from the trammels of the publishing world and its conformity, though they are sometimes tampered with by well-meaning missionaries, who seek to direct the writing into innocent bland stories.

If a strong literature based on Aboriginal forms is to develop, the place for this development is among people least affected by assimilation, and once an upsurge of literature begins it is only a matter of conjecture where it may lead. In fact future Aborigines may look back on this present settlement literature as having a lost simplicity, or a complexity only brought out through a deep reading of the text. Magabala Books has a number of manuscripts developed from such texts. It is these that may go towards creating a new Aboriginal literature away from the Metropolitan tradition.

2

Fringe and Metropolitan

RENÉ WELLEK AND AUSTIN WARREN IN THEIR *THEORY of Literature* (1973, p. 34) have this to say about literatures which do not belong to what is called the 'grand' or 'Metropolitan' tradition of literature as formulated in Europe:

> There seems to be a thin line between 'committed' literature, that is literature coming from a certain community and giving voice to its needs, and protest literature. When communities are under stress, that line is often crossed and there is a tendency to dismiss 'protest' as propaganda, that is we reject it as poetry or label as mere rhetoric everything that persuades us to a definite outward action.

Their words set out the overall tendency of most books stemming from the metropolitan centres of literature (and in 'Metropolitan', I include Australian critics and writers) to postulate that there is only one poetry, one literature comparable to all ages, and this is the Western canon. By doing this, by pursuing this line, they relegate all other literatures to the fringe, except for those authors in good standing, and by this I mean those who produce works which approximate most to what the Metropolitan critics consider literature should be. This extends even to those fringe writers who utilise supposedly the oral traditions of their communities.

Unfortunately, often the Metropolitan critics taken up with the very seriousness of their field are enraged or led astray by fringe authors who play on their susceptibilities by using their tradition against itself. I refer here to such tricksters as Yambo Ouologuem who constructing a novel out of the very debris of Metropolitan literature was hailed as the new genius of African literature until the extent of his borrowings became known, and the Samoan writer, Albert Wendt who, in his novel, *Leaves of the Banyan Tree*, utilised a particular form of English which was hailed as stemming, or rushing straight from the villages of the islands onto his typewriter. Unfortunately this was not the case, and the dialect of his prose came directly from his mind.

In both these cases, Metropolitan critics are able through the use of argument and the control of the critical apparatus to squirm out of such *faux pas* as they themselves commit. Reputations are not often lost in the field of literary critical studies. Perhaps what is needed is the eyes to see literature as a joke, that the very opacity of a language is fine for wordplay, but not for truth-telling, that there is no such thing as good or bad literature, but only language which stems from a particular language-group who use literature genres, when the need arises, as ready made forms to fit what they want to say, or if individuals feel the very 'joking-ness' of literature. This is the position of Augusto Boal in his *Theater of the Oppressed* (1979). I refer here also to the idiosyncratic poems of a Lionel Fogarty who mixes prose and poetry to bring into disrepute the very nature of poetry.

What must be admitted, even if the jokingness of liter-ature is not, is that the value of literature has steadily decreased until it has become only an item on the shelves of the supermarket. Poetry, even though critics continue to stress its importance, has escaped this fate by its very unimportance, at least as printed text. Without economic value it is left to flounder, or to be torn over by critics. What is good, bad, or indifferent is left to be fought over in conferences and the hall of academia, and the general public remains unmoved, except in those communities where poetry is a living force, rather than something which receives value because we are told so in schools.

Aboriginal literature as a literature of the fringe does not belong to the Metropolitan tradition, or does it? This is a matter of contention, for example when teaching Aboriginal literature, students have drawn my attention to the styles of *Wandering Girl* and *My Place* as lying respectively in such popular women's genre as 'Mills and Boon' and 'gothic romances'. Apart from this, the metropolitan literary tradition, or at least those aspects considered suitable for children and young adults, is taught in schools.

The poetry we were exposed to as victims of assimilation were the ballads and metred rhymes of such word formations as 'I love a sunburnt country'. We, under the assimilation policy, were forced to participate in the acculturation process before dropping away and out, only venturing into the realms of higher education in the last decade or so. Thus, it is only reasonable to assume that if and when Aborigines began writing, we would use such forms we had learnt to be poetry in these schools, though this is not to downplay other cultural inputs like music, such as country and western, or remnant Aboriginal songs, or the speech-patterns of our communities, or the oral traditions which linger on, though downplayed in the schools, where Jacky and Mary were to be civilised. I leave aside here such popular literatures as romances and detective stories with only the comment that Carter Browne is as important to my literary development as Sartre and Camus.

The assimilation policy introduced Aborigines to the Metropolitan tradition in the form of ballads and other so-called simple verse structures which resulted in poets such as Oodgeroo Noonuccal and Jack Davis producing metred and rhymed verse. Usually, they did not go on to read modern poets in good standing in the tradition, but returned to their Aboriginal roots, or ventured into the realms of African or Afro-American poetry, or even into Asian poetry where metre and rhythm continue to be used. The later experiments of the Metropolitan tradition were ignored, or found unfitted to Aboriginality. This meant that critics could dismiss Aboriginal poetry as derivative and bad. Thus, Australian anthologies firmly wedded to the European tradition could ignore Aboriginal poetry in English, or pay word-service and slip one into the beginning of the volume to show that after all they, as Australians, recognised the indigenes as part of Australia, though they wished that they would write poetry more akin to their own. Aboriginal writers in turn could dismiss white Australian poetry, except for those with subject matter similar to our own, as not worth reading. After all, it had little communal value, and if poetry was necessary, there were other fringe literatures to read which were similar to our own.

Written Aboriginal literature, except for a few retellings of legends and stories, arose at a particular time in Aboriginal history. In the mid-sixties Oodgeroo Noonuccal's first book of poems, *We Are Going*, was published to the consternation of critics who dismissed it as (what else?) fringe literature.

My novel, *Wildcat Falling*, heavily edited and launched with a foreword which in effect said that assimilation was working in that now 'they' can write novels just as 'they' can paint watercolours, was well received. It followed to a great extent the Metropolitan tradition with the hallmarks of character development, supposedly a feature of the then modern novels. The unnamed character advanced into the arms of the police and the ending provided the hope that he might eventually settle down, or be assimilated into the wider Australian society if given the necessary help.

This more or less paralleled Oodgeroo's poems which also asked for help, though these were not so well received owing to both content and form. But, in spite of the critics, they sold well enough for her publishers to accept another of her collections of poetry, *The Dawn Is At Hand*. This too sold well, and both were collected into a volume, *My People* which has been in print to this day.

In some ways literature, apart from being a joke, is also a prophecy. Oodgeroo Noonuccal's poems foreshadowed the emancipation of the Aborigines, citizenship rights, freedom rides, and eventually the land rights struggle. She was in the forefront of all these movements, and her poetry grew with them. Her poems have been condemned for being political tracts, which they are, but in the Aboriginal tradition, a tradition reflected by many other fringe peoples, there is no fault in this.

In Aboriginal poetry, it is the message which is supreme, with any aesthetic appeal being of lesser worth. Thus, there arises in those critics embedded in the Metropolitan tradition a contradiction between message-value and aesthetic-value, and as most critics tend to be on the side of aesthetic-value, they easily dismiss such verse as not being in the realms of poetry. Naturally, as they have created this tradition, they select what is and what is not acceptable, especially as it pertains to such things as the use of ordered rhymes and rhythms as found in the Western folk tradition. This in modern and postmodern poetry is not to be used seriously; is to be alluded to, or even subverted. After all as a form it is *passé*.

What lurks behind such suppositions of course is the reliance on genre definition to break literature into different categories. These are accepted as to what constitutes such things as poetry with the convention that poetry is supposed to be written in ragged lines, and that lines of prose are neatly justified to the right and left: a centralist position if ever there was one. A further convention is that poetic language must be based on imagery which leads to an obscurity of language centred on a theme to be deciphered at one's leisure.

Poetry is an arcane subject, or rather an arcane set of signifiers to be meditated upon in the privacy of one's study, or library. It definitely is not to be screamed out in a political meeting. Thus Dennis Rasmussen in his *Poetry and Truth* (1975, p. 25) differentiates poetry from other forms of discourse in that a non-poetic composition has a use or function, while a poem has no use or function beyond a fidelity to its own nature. This may be the case in the Metropolitan tradition, but not in Aboriginal poetry where the aesthetic value or function is not dominant.

Aboriginal poetry may be defined as a verbal discourse in which the message is dominant and the aesthetic function is subordinate. Aboriginal poetry, and I am talking here of the type of poetry written by Oodgeroo Noonuccal and Jack Davis, is best defined by semiology.

Semiology is the science that studies the life of signs in a society, and language may be seen as a social semiotic.

Language arises in the life of an individual from childhood through an ongoing exchange of meanings between members of a community. A community itself may be seen as a semiotic construct, or a system of signs which forms the culture of a particular community. Members of a community exchange information and goods and services through the dynamic interplay of speech roles. Not only this, but through their speech and the patterns of their speech (discourse) they act out their own status and roles, establishing and transmitting their shared systems of values and knowledge. A community is thus bound together in a system of signs which all members share, but when a minority community wishes to communicate with a majority community, this system of signs may break down. There may be an incomprehension between the two groups. It is then that writers find a niche in formulating sign-systems which may readily be understood by both communities.

Thus Oodgeroo Noonuccal and Jack Davis to get their message across to the majority community, rely on the past sign systems of the majority community which are accepted as being poetic. Here, it must be borne in mind that the system of signs accepted by many as signifying poetic discourse, or being recognised as poetry, is rhymed verse, and so both poets produce this type of verse to get through to the maximum number of people. As a strategy, this has proved sucessful as the sales of Oodgeroo Noonuccal's (Kath Walker) book, *My People* show.

Aesthetic value is subordinated to content, or message value. This is clearly stated by Oodgeroo Noonuccal in a 1977 interview with Jim Davidson in *Meanjin*:

> Oh yes, oh yes. I'm putting their voices on paper, writing their things. I listen to the Aboriginal people, to their cry for help—it was more or less a cry for help in that first book: *We Are Going*. I don't consider it my book, it was the people.

Apart from the importance of message over aesthetics, Oodgeroo shows that she takes a community approach to literature and to poetics. What this means is that it is the aesthetics of the poet's community which determines the aesthetic ground of her work. It is no use seeking to be highly experimental if one ends up with no readers and it is a fact that the critical censure of the community given orally at various meetings influences the work of the Aboriginal writer.

The Aboriginal writer does not exist in isolation, but as a member of the community who see, or attach certain values to his or her literary production. One of these values is the criterion of worth. Thus any individual preoccupations, say for example with the extremes of sexuality, is dismissed. Often a criterion of value is the degree of Aboriginality in the work. This is becoming of increasing importance in that as more and more Aborigines become educated, they are exposed to other forms of poetry than the rhythmic rhymes of the bush ballad. It is then that Aboriginality comes to the fore, and the complex poems of a poet like Lionel Fogarty are read.

His poems do not rely on a primary school implanted appreciation of poetry, but strike new ground in being deeply rooted in both form and content in Aboriginality. This in itself may be a problem in that the sign system of his Murri community is not that of the majority community, and that a white reader may be put off by the strangeness of his system of signs. In effect an understanding of his verse relies on an understanding of the cultural system structured within it. This reality is different from that of the European.

Aboriginal reality is different from white reality in that it is an expanded reality akin to the dreaming life. In fact in traditional Aboriginal society, the dreaming of literary works such as the Ngurlu of the Kimberley region of Western Australia is the accepted form of literary creation. Songs and rituals are not brain-made, but imparted in dreams. They in effect are passed on, and this is the method of composition of Lionel Fogarty.

The process is akin to European surrealism, which sought inspiration from the unconscious. Lionel Fogarty uses surrealistic techniques to get at the very underlying stuff of Aboriginality residing in the condensed and concentrated obsessions of the unconscious, or the individual dreaming.

His poetry arises as a response to an individual need which gives it an exact definition, and this may be compared to the works of some traditional poets and songmen, for example Butcher Joe Nangan whose Ngurlu lines of song verse deal with the death and burial of his mother.

It is precisely in surrealism, or the reliance on dreaming techniques to bring forth literary works, a traditional method of creation, that Aboriginal poetry may retreat from the assimilation situation of the primary school and into an authentic Aboriginality, opposed to assimilation and foreign formats. The aim is to destroy the type of poetry directed at the majority community by poets such as Jack Davis and Oodgeroo Noonuccal and to replace it with the desires in the shape of language and structure which are found in the depths of Aboriginal being. This method is a directed mode of automatic writing, not because there is the intervention of reflection, but because words and images constantly and continually express the same obsessions lying at the basis of individual Aboriginal existence in Australia. This type of poetry, utterly 'committed', expresses what poetry (at least in Western literary theory) should not do, that is give a situational, social and political importance to the genre.

3

Ignoring the Fringe

A REVIEW OF OODGEROO NOONUCCAL'S (KATH WALKER) first book of poetry appearing in *Overland* (1967, p. 4) casually dismissed her work in these words:

> If I had my way I would ban all publishers' blurbs. Apart from their inaccuracy, the dust jacket comments on *The Dawn Is At Hand* do Kath Walker a disservice. She is no poet, and her verse is not poetry in any true sense. It hasn't that serious commitment to formal rightness, that concern for making speech true under all circumstances, which distinguishes Buckley and Wright at their best. *The Dawn Is At Hand* belongs more rightly to that field of social protest in which Miss Walker's statements are most relevant and most moving. I have a sincere respect for her indignation, her sense of pathos, and her forthright candour. For any white Australian with a conscience her book is often moving and shaming. But to invite us to approach it as poetry is to invite us to take the easy way out, to avoid its message (for it is a book with a message) by measuring it against standards and preoccupations with which it has really little to do.

Few volumes of poetry receive such scathing criticism. It only goes to show the strength of Oodgeroo that she continued to write poetry and to achieve the distinction of being Australia's best selling poet after C. J. Dennis. The above dismissal is tempered only by the leftist humanist tradition, then still strong among members of the Anglo-Celtic literary establishment. This meant that although the cause of the poor Aborigines had to be respected, this respect could not be extended to their poetry. In the service of aesthetics it had to be dismissed out of hand. For one thing it was too simple and direct, and poetry should be anything but this.

It is interesting that this review, by Andrew Taylor, begins with a short sentence in which the reviewer wishes that he could assume the role of dictator and ban Kath Walker's verse as poetry. His solution as to what genre it should be placed in, as Aborigines are the objects of study by anthropologists and sociologists, is the non-literary field of social protest. His message is very similar to the racist comment that Aborigines are all right as long as they stay in their place, but Oodgeroo was refusing to stay in her place. She was extending the Aboriginal struggle for equal rights and justice into the arena of literature, knocking on the doors of the Anglo-Celtic literary establishment with verse often as simple as a fist. They refused to open their doors and dismissed her as a poor Aborigine whose voice should not be heard in their neighbourhood. The place of a fringe dweller is on the fringe.

Most poetry is polysemic in nature and on a deep reading yields more than a single meaning. If this is kept in mind we may advance to a deeper understanding of some of Oodgeroo's verse. An example would be her short poem 'My Love'.

> Possess me? No, I cannot give
> The love that others know,
> For I am wedded to a cause:
> The rest I must forgo.
>
> You claim me as your very own,
> My body, soul and mind;
> My love is my own people first,
> And after that, mankind.

The social part, the personal
I have renounced of old;
Mine is a dedicated life,
No man's to have and hold.

Old white intolerance hems me round,
Insult and scorn assail;
I must be free, I must be strong
To fight and not to fail.

For there are ancient wrongs to right,
Men's malice to endure;
A long road and a lonely road,
But oh, the goal is sure.

> Oodgeroo of the Tribe Noonuccal
> (formerly Kath Walker)

The title is ambiguous in itself: does it mean 'To my love', or 'what my love is', or 'what man's love is'? The first stanza begins with the question, 'Possess Me?' And the rest of the stanza is taken up with the reply which even on a second reading is very obscure, except if we take the definite 'No' after 'Possess Me?', to be a refusal to a certain type of possessive love, though in the rest of the sentence there is an implied opposition in that the poet is the one who is renouncing the possession, with a further implication that being wedded to a cause is an excuse for forgoing the rest.

The second stanza is made up of two oppositions: the possessive partner, and the poet's reply, with the final 'mankind', implying that it is a man she is writing about, though again we should keep in mind the ambiguity of the title 'My Love', in the sense of 'This is how I love, and the passive is not for me.' The fourth stanza follows the rhythmic pattern of two joined couplets with the same sort of opposition implied between first and last couplet. The surface structure of the poem is a stylised response and answer, with the first couplet giving what the poet sees as negative aspects of love, or desire, and the second couplet replying to it.

What are these negative traits?: possession, claiming, the personal, white intolerance, man's malice. These are opposed to wedded, love, dedicated, free (strong, fight) and the final goal. Although published in 1964, the poem is interesting in that it is (among other things) a paean of praise to the independent woman. It ends on a note of affirmation rather than decrying the fact that the poet cannot give herself in a personal relationship. The poem says more than I receive in my first superficial reading, which was that the poet was simply decrying the fact that her commitment has denied her a true love that will last forever of the 'possess me I am yours' variety. A deeper reading reveals that she is criticising the subservient place of woman in a patriarchal love-relationship.

Thus Oodgeroo's poetry often condemned for being simple and trite is really a condemnation of all superficial first readings. However, there may be more substance in the criticism that if Aboriginal creative writing is to thrive as a separate entity it must be independent as much as possible from white Australian influence, and that Oodgeroo's poetry owing to its reliance on the bush ballad format is betraying its Aboriginality.

This may be true if it is ignored that 'message' is placed above aesthetics. It must also be tempered with the fact that a fringe minority is an encapsulated minority. It is surrounded by the majority culture and though it exists on the fringes, the majority influences are so great that it is almost impossible to escape them. Thus the strong rhythms of the ballad, the iambic metre with its accent on the second syllable as in Aboriginal clapstick playing, have come to influence the verse of Oodgeroo, though this is not to imply that all her verse is in this form. Again, strong rhythm is a necessity for the recitation of poetry, and Oodgeroo's poetry is meant to be recited, is meant to be heard. It is the rhythm of the metre which carries the words. When I listen to contemporary black poetry I am always aware of the rhythm. The words lean on it and are carried by it. They are a joy to listen to, though with a silent reading I may find the words trite.

Often it is assumed by Europeans that there is a single and unified Aboriginal response to white dominance in

Australia. This is far from true, and the ambiguity and divisiveness in the response is mirrored in the discourse structures of Aboriginal poets. Oodgeroo's verse discourse veers from the Aboriginality of 'The Bunyip' with the rhythm of the lines once removed from Kriol to 'We Are Going' in a straight English addressing itself to the white reader and those Aborigines completely at home in standard English. There is little sign of Aboriginality in these English lines, though I am aware as Bruce McGuinness points out in his paper in *Aboriginal Writing Today* (p. 47):

> When Aboriginal people write they write in a style. They're able to adopt various styles of writing so what they really want to write about is hidden. It's contained within their writing. They become actors in fact.

But we may query whether the effect is worth it, if the result is to be dismissed? If the need is to be published in order to get the message across this is legitimate, though dangerous, for it leaves Aboriginal writers open to subversion in that as white people view their literature in certain ways they will seek to impose their concepts on to Aboriginal writing. It will be those texts which correspond closely to the Metropolitan canons of literature which will be accepted. In this regard, it is the Aboriginal novel following closely, or copying these canons, which is accepted much more than poetry.

The Anglo-Celtic majority culture seeks to condition and explain Aboriginal literature through its own expectations. It dominates the economic and cultural institutions of Australia and too often it is its voice which is heard, not Aboriginal voices. In the case of Oodgeroo Noonuccal and Jack Davis, their verse is judged by western standards and found wanting. This approach is not only invalid in presupposing that there is an absolute artistic standard which is identical with the Western standard, or that the poets are writing verse for aesthetic enjoyment, but it also is an active agent in suppressing any development of Aboriginal arts which lie outside this standard.

Thus good Aboriginal literature is taken to be that which

approximates Western literature, and especially in contemporary literary theory those texts which stand by themselves away from the author and deal with what are regarded as universal themes. Opposite to this is the view which accepts Aboriginal poetry as being occasional verse and reads it, as in the case of Oodgeroo's 'My Love' as a simple dedication to a cause rather than a refusal to accept the Anglo-Celtic standards of patriarchal love, and thus an affirmation of the love-relationship akin to the traditional Aboriginal independent sex roles of men and women.

What must be kept in mind is that the primary criticism of Aboriginal arts and literature must come from Aborigines, and what must be rejected is a white interference which threatens not only the independence of the text, but the producer of the text. This does not mean that Aboriginal works must not be criticised harshly, or that Western critical standards based on an objective literary theory must not be used; but if these standards are used, we must be fully conscious of their development.

Western critical standards and theories are developed in the Western tradition and are applied by critics to interpret and criticise Western literature for the Western audience. Thus, when the black critic Cliff Watego stated in his paper given at the First Aboriginal Writers Conference and published in *Aboriginal Writing Today* that Oodgeroo Noonuccal had been heavily influenced by Henry Lawson, he immediately invoked a whole concept of Lawsonism with which Anglo-Celtic readers are acquainted as part of their cultural education.

Most Aborigines until recently having had only a primary school education are out of this tradition, or if knowing it, reject Henry Lawson because of his stated racism. We are repelled when the non-racist Oodgeroo Noonuccal is compared to him. Cliff Watego did not take into account that when Anglo-Celtic critics review Aboriginal writing they immediately try to compare it with white Australian works. They rarely seek to establish parallels with for example, traditional Aboriginal song-texts such as the tyabi. Usually, this is because they are innocent of any knowledge of pre-Invasion Australian poetry, but if they do seek to use

Aboriginal sources they are content to refer back to the producer of the text and his or her assumed knowledge or lack of knowledge of traditional Aboriginal culture.

Some white critics have noticed how such poets as Jack Davis, Kevin Gilbert and Oodgeroo Noonuccal by their use of white forms are showing that they are victims of government policies. These policies of enforced assimilation changed their whole creative output. By preventing access to their culture, by denying them the free use of a variety of Aboriginal poem types, it was assured that what culture they were exposed to would be Anglo-Celtic. It was only natural that when they decided to express themselves they did so through these forms. It is only recently with the growth and consolidation of Aboriginality that a new generation of writers have started to produce a literature vastly different from the assimilationist models.

Still, I remain aware that cultural genocide is still a potent force in Australia. We Aboriginal writers must be aware and remain aware that if we choose to use white forms we are in effect 'thinking white'; that by using these forms we are leaving ourselves open to be judged purely by white standards. And this often means:

> The techniques of Kath Walker's poetry are the unsophisticated ones of the bush balladists. It is to be expected that her reviewer in the *Times Literary Supplement* should write: 'At times the metres of her poems are trite, stemming from the worst type of nineteenth century hymns'. This is undoubtedly true. Kath Walker is hardly to be expected to have a rich background in European poetry. As a child she would most likely have been exposed to little other verse than 'the worst type of nineteenth century hymn', and her mother, as she tells us in the dedication of the poem 'The Teachers', was illiterate. She is not in a position to have a very sensitive appreciation of European verse rhythms, but at the same time she cannot use the structure and techniques of the poetry of her Aboriginal ancestors.

It is all very well for Ruth Doobov to write this in her article on Oodgeroo Noonuccal (*Australian Literary Studies*

6 (1), 1973), but we might spare a thought to consider what would happen if Oodgeroo did use the structure and techniques of her Aboriginal culture. What would be the critic's reaction to them?

When I submitted my collection of poetry, *The Song Circle of Jacky*, (1986) to a publisher, it was sent on to a reader, which is normal practice. The reader commented that the incantatory repetitions of traditional Aboriginal songs without their musical accompaniment become boring on the page. And if we seek other critical opinions on more experimental poems, such as those by Bobbi Sykes in her volume, *Love Poems and Other Revolutionary Actions* (1979), we find that they are dismissed for not being poetry.

And so it appears that Aboriginal poetry is condemned for being trite, if not trite then boring, if not boring, then not poetry. It often is a case of 'Go away', and if Aboriginal poems are needed for anthologies, then they are selected from translations of traditonal song cycles done by anthropologists. In the *New Oxford Book of Australian Verse* (1986) extracts from the taped accounts of the oral tradition of the Mowanjum community have been published as Aboriginal poetry. This is not so, for the contents of the tape was long after rendered into a poetic form to bring out its spiritual message by Sydney poet, Andrew Huntley.

This brings into question what exactly is Aboriginal poetry and perhaps what is poetry? Be that as it may, I accept that the majority culture have the right to include whatever poems they wish to in their anthologies, subject to permission of the owners, but what I find verging on dishonesty is the inclusion of texts from white sources and then the labelling of them as Aboriginal, rather than Aboriginal-derived. What is also of importance is the question of royalties? Does the Aboriginal poet, or oral storyteller get any royalties for his or her work?

Aboriginal culture is becoming a national resource with anyone taking whatever they wish from it. I know that this is part of postmodernism, that in our multicultural world everything not subject to copyright is there to be poached. Aboriginal culture especially in the bicentennial year of 1988 was used by everyone from tee-shirt manufacturers to doll makers. It is difficult to see how this can be stopped unless Aboriginal designs are copyrighted. The 'look and feel' court cases recently settled in favour of computer software manufacturers may be extended to Aboriginal arts and crafts. In the past, anthropologists and others collected a mass of oral material which is now owned by them. The traditional owner, in anthropological circles called 'the informant' has no claim on this material. Translations made from it do not belong to him or her. Often their names are not even acknowledged. As part of the good work being done by the Australian Institute of Aboriginal Studies, ownership now remains with the original creators and owners. This is because the Institute funds much research and can stipulate conditions governing that research. Perhaps the next step would be for the Institute to initiate 'look and feel' litigation against those who steal Aboriginal cultural designs and products.

Translations from oral sources still appear in anthologies of Australian verse and without any direct acknowledgement of the Aboriginal owner of such material. It is as if they exist in a primordial wilderness, or a primitive Communist Utopia where private ownership does not exist. This owes more to Engels than to reality. It may be said that individuals belonging to a particular clan hold a song cycle in common. Each member has a version, or a part of that song cycle, and each version, or part is privately owned.

Aborigines are caught in a web from which we must extricate ourselves. It is little use calling for an independent literature when over the last year, 1988, many Aboriginal books published were cooperative efforts between Aborigines and Europeans. In one case brought to my knowledge by the writer this was to her detriment. At least there has been progress. The Aboriginal writer, or storyteller is given his or her due share of acknowledgement.

Another problem is that if you write a book and submit it to a publisher it is difficult not to have it placed in the hands of an editor. In the fifties and early sixties, in the majority culture there was much debate about whether a writer should have an editor, or should allow his works to be edited. Those who stood for the independence of the writer lost the argument and now not only are books edited, but even individual poems. Thus creativity is a collective effort and this will most likely remain so even in Aboriginal publishing houses. I may ask how does this affect the *Aboriginality* of a work? It is difficult to provide an answer. The term itself is even difficult to define. The term, Aboriginality has arisen because it provides an ideology by which Aboriginal literature may be judged. It is much more than this however, for it provides a lifeline by which dissociated individuals may be pulled back to their matrical essence. It is the promise of a coming-into-being of not only an Aboriginal aesthetics, but of new social entities which will reflect the underlying humaneness of Aboriginal being. Essentially, it is not a static ideology based on fixed traditional ways of expression and culture, but is as Kevin Gilbert declares in his introduction to *Living Black* (1978) a way of building a contemporary Aboriginal culture, a radical re-education of Aborigines by Aborigines and at the direction of Aborigines.

4

Reading the Fringe

To understand Aboriginal writers such as Jack Davis, Oodgeroo Noonuccal, Kevin Gilbert and myself, it must be understood that we are representatives of a generation scarred by assimilation. This fact, this government policy, dominated our lives. White Australian writers have always had freedom. It has been their birthright, but for the Aboriginal people there has always been the government over them, the various departments of Aboriginal Affairs, the police and, in extreme cases, the army. This is still fact as recent events and the overwhelming Aboriginal prison population bear out.

Freedom is not the birthright of the Australian Aborigine. If he ends up at the receiving end of white law, he is never treated as a gentleman, or even a common Australian citizen, but as a 'boong'. A member of a minority community to be kept firmly in place, to be escorted to the native camp, to the fringe and left there to rot in poverty and squalor. The whole of white Australian history has been the denial of freedom to the Aboriginal people. It has denied them any history or right of expression. Under the gaze of the 'white other' they wilt, or revolt and die, or seek for some understanding by using the techniques of the white culture which oppresses them. But by using these techniques, by giving them a legitimacy in the Aboriginal world, we affirm them.

Aboriginal poets by using the verse structures of Europe have given them an importance in Aboriginal thought. They have provided models of verse structure which other Aboriginal poets may use. This means in practice that these poets can be judged according to the European tradition. It is only when we come to the newer generation of poets such as Lionel Fogarty that the critical assumptions of Europe break down. Critics are either forced to condemn outright, or attempt to arrive at some understanding by utilising their theory, and to modify it to arrive at new ways of seeing and understanding.

To attempt a deep reading of Lionel Fogarty is to penetrate into a world divorced from the European and to come to some understanding of an Australian reality, or discourse which exists only on the fringe of white consciousness in heavy academic books or infrequent newspaper articles. Lionel Fogarty is the forerunner of those Aboriginal poets who seek to establish a discourse of Aboriginality not based on European patterns and, in refusing to be sucked in by those patterns, his verse at times approaches the surrealism of African writers such as Cesaire or Senghor, though fractured and changed by the blight of Australia. Even the Aboriginal writers of the sixties often have problems in coming to grips with his verse. It is not the product of assimilation and lacks that precision of meaning found in much of the verse of Oodgeroo Noonuccal and Jack Davis. We are unfamiliar with his style of writing; but is it to be condemned because we are still trapped by what we learnt in primary schools?

A true poet, Lionel Fogarty wrestles with words to produce Aboriginal verse which is difficult for many readers to accept. There are only two ways to approach Lionel. He is to be dismissed, or accepted as a major poet. I consider him one of the most original poets of Australia, though I accept that his works can be difficult. But what we as readers must understand is that we are reading the works of a poet in which there is not only the evidence of a rape of the Aboriginal soul, but the healing of the soul.

In his works Aboriginal literature escapes the confines of Europe and frees itself of European patterns and concerns. An original voice has emerged to sing of the sad wounds inflicted on a whole people, of hundreds of mouths forced into shaping the harsh sounds of an alien speech so unlike the liquid Aboriginal discourse patterns:

> If I don't succeed, bear with me,
> I see words beyond any acceptable meaning
> And this is how I express my dreaming . . .

The language of poetry differs from everyday usage and great poets wrestle with the language in an effort to put into words their visions. Lionel Fogarty does not accept language as he finds it; but displaces and distorts grammar and syntax in an effort to create a new meaning. Displacing is used by Lionel to shift white meaning to black meaning. In his poem, 'Pitjantajara Be Us' (*Yoogum Yoogum* 1982, p. 85), there is the line '*So come on down/and freehold us*'. 'Freehold' is a term which refers to land, for example, 'freehold title', and can be taken as referring to the struggle for land by the Aborigines; but in his usage the meaning has been changed to emphasise the oneness between the Pitjantajara people and their land. To free the land in effect means to free the people; and to free the people means to free the land. There can be no freedom for the people unless there are land rights. Thus by a simple displacing of meaning he evokes the spirituality implicit in the land rights movement.

It is difficult to separate individual lines out of a text to elicit separate meanings, for Lionel's poems have a unity that defies this approach. His poem, 'Free Our Dreams' (*Yoogum Yoogum*, p. 87) is a fine example of his work:

> Out of the hole we came out of a hole
>   filled with poles of unfolded reasons
> As it flies past
>   songs came off in blood
> We find strength to be blue and red
>   ride it to expansion
> Yet you people miss what they came as
>   miss everything living that lives for
> Power

> Don't give them the human power
> that makes green frogs cut open for enjoyment
> Make it the kind of compassion
> for establishment rules on love
> Smelling noises
> of burning fingertips
> Water came falling
> Like digesting loud rushing pains
> Eaten a sickly sight of spirituality.
>
> Treat us to a barking laughter
> like running creeks
> speared out for swimming fish
> dead leaves, dead weeds go with our seeds
> Roots grown out
> mingled with shining desire
>
> Free our dreams.

Here Lionel uses distortion to create ambiguity and contradiction. He uses textual space as a principle of organisation for making signs out of linguistic items which may not be meaningful otherwise. We might ask what do these devices do in his poetry? There is but one answer—that they threaten the literary representation of reality, or mimesis.

As readers, we expect to be presented with a context consistent with what we believe to be reality. Usually, this reality reflects what we see around us. It is the true as opposed to the untrue, and grammar and discourse are supposed to reflect this especially if we accept that language and reality are identical. This is the position of early Aboriginal poetry. It claims to give a correct picture of the Aboriginal condition in Australia, that is reality. What we perceive or conceive around us is identified with the words we read. We often ignore the fact that words and verse structures are mere signs signifying this reality. A deeper understanding of these signs breaks up this simple signification and what we then read is not objective reality, but the effect assimilation has had on Aboriginal writers.

These signs can be read in three ways. Firstly as an exposition of the Aboriginal condition in Australia; secondly as the effect of assimilation on the individual poet, and thirdly merely as verse, either good, bad, or indifferent. It is the third reading which has led to a rejection of such poetry. Aesthetically, it was considered not good enough to be ranked with first class poetry, that is the poetry of the Metropolitan tradition, though the poet's often stated aim was to mirror the Aboriginal condition.

The basic characteristic of this mirroring of reality (mimesis) is that it must produce a continuously changing semantic sequence to create a direct relationship of words to things. That is, the text multiplies details and keeps shifting its focus to achieve an acceptable likeness to reality. A rather complex use of this shifting of focus is in Jack Davis' 'Tribal Man in the City' where each line of the poem begins with the signifier 'Black' followed by a definition which makes the reality of the tribal man in the city black indeed. The poem is grammatically laid out and there is none of the ungrammaticalities as found in Lionel's work, as given above. These are noticed by the reader from the first. They eventually lead him or her to perceive that this common trait forms them into a paradigm which alters the meaning of the poem and allows for polysemic contrast. For example in the given poem the first stanza stresses Aboriginal power based on ritual, then opposes it to the power of 'you people', then reiterates Aboriginal power as residing in nature.

The ungrammaticalities of Lionel's poem signify components in a network of relationships. It is here that the approach of the unsophisticated critic breaks down. The reader does not advance beyond a first reading in which an attempt is made to decode the poem from the beginning to the end of the text. He or she attempts to apprehend meaning using his or her linguistic competence which includes an assumption that language is referential, and that words do indeed relate to things.

The reader also perceives incompatibilities between words, recognises that a word or phrase does not make sense, that semantic transfers are there, and that a deciphering of the single, linear text is necessary for the perception of irony or humour, or what have you. But this reader input occurs only because he or she has the necessary linguistic competence to perceive ungrammaticalities. It is impossible to bypass them, for they are in the text and must be dealt with. This occurs on the grammatical level, and grammar is important in that in many of Lionel's poems it is the grammatical use of Aboriginal English which acts as a signifier for Aborigines. There is a twofold grammar at work which tends to mix up the signs so that what may seem obscure to a white reader will be clear to an Aboriginal one. Again there is a further level in that the descriptive systems, the themes, the mythology employed, may be outside the white reader's familiarity.

An inability to get at a meaning, or to fully comprehend the poem necessitates a second or retroactive reading. As the reader progresses again through the text, he or she remembers what has been read, and modifies understanding in the light of what is now being decoded. As progress is made through the text, there is a reviewing, a revising, a comparing backwards and forwards as the structure is decoded, though as language is a social semiotic of a particular community, this may not be enough. In fact the reader may have to go outside the text to gather information in order to decipher it.

Lionel Fogarty has written five volumes of verse: *Kargun* (1980), *Yoogum Yoogum* (1982), *Kudjela* (1983), *Ngutji* (1984) and *Jagera* (forthcoming). To enter into his poetry, it is best to read the entire five volumes in order of production. In this way the earlier codes in *Kargun* which seem difficult at first or second reading may be decoded from the later texts. *Kargun* itself may then be used as a key to decipher the later poems of *Kudjela*, *Ngutji* and *Jagera*. Thus what in *Kargun* were noticed as ungrammaticalities begin to appear as variants of a basic logical language structuring Aboriginality, and the sustained relationship of each text to this structure of Aboriginality enables the reader to decode the individual poems.

It is a tenet of modern Western criticism that a poem is a

single unit and should be read as such. I believe that in Lionel's case, the underlying structure of Aboriginality is of paramount importance, and that if we do not accept this, his poetry may be indecipherable. This is not to diminish any conventional reading of a single poem as a unity, but to gain the maximum effect from a retroactive reading, we must understand that the climax of its function as a generator of significance lies in perceiving the underlying structure as being formed from a unifying experience of Aboriginality.

I emphasise that a hindrance towards experiencing the fullness of Lionel's work is to take each poem as an individual text to be solely deciphered or decoded. The individual text must be seen as part of a complex network of Aboriginality which in effect transcends any simple reading. Perhaps this will become clear if we take the single poem I have given before. I repeat the poem here so that readers may engage in a second reading:

FREE OUR DREAMS

Out of a hole we came out of a hole
    filled with poles of unfolded reasons
As it flies past
    songs came off in blood
We find strength to be blue and red
    ride it to expansion
Yet you people miss what they came as
    miss everything living that lives for
Power.

Don't give then the human power
    that makes green frogs cut open for enjoyment
Make it the kind of compassion
    for establishment rules on love
Smelling noises
    of burning finger tips
Water came falling
    Like digesting loud rushing pains
Eaten a sickly sight of spirituality.

Treat us to a barking laughter
like running creeks
speared out for swimming fish
dead leaves, dead weeds go with our seeds
Roots grown out
mingled with shining desire

Free our dreams.

In our first reading, we became aware that we were not in the literal world of descriptive signs, or of mimesis. In that first reading, we were forced to transcend any checking of language with perceived reality. In a second reading we notice that there is not a shift towards symbolism, but a symbolism implicit from the first line, and oppositions which must be deciphered. 'Holes' are opposed to 'poles', reduced to a pole, perhaps a penis expanding, referring back to the 'hole' which may be equated to the vagina, the womb pregnant with life, with power. Thus what may seem at first to be simple oppositions of hole to pole is deciphered into a relationship of hole/vagina, pole/penis, birthing into songs, strength, expansion; all forms of positiveness, of fecundity, of creativity opposed, in the last lines of the stanza, to people lacking this power.

The chief sign in the first stanza is *power*. Signs are never isolated, but exist in a relationship within a system be it the poem or the meta-poem of Aboriginality. Thus this power may be seen to refer back to we, the Aborigines, who know our origins, who know our power which in the Aboriginal meta-structure is the earth thus extending our first hole/vagina symbolism to include a literal hole in the earth. Again our pole/penis symbolism in the light of the meta-structure may now extend to the 'rangga' poles of initiation, or of power bestowing a meaning strengthened by songs and blood, components of Aboriginal ritual, with the 'flying pole' referring to the clever men of Aboriginal culture who use such an item to fly through the air. This is where power resides and it is precisely this power which is missed by 'you people' (referring to the white people). Thus in this first stanza the signs make sense only if treated by using the meta-poem or text of Aboriginality. It is then that the reasons unfold as the magician flies past on his wand.

The significance of a poem is more than or something other than the total meaning deducible from a comparison between the variants within its structure. Significance is the practice of transformation, of change, realisation akin to the play of children, or the acting out of ritual. Thus, in Lionel's poem there is a circuitous sequencing, a way of using language which keeps revolving around a key word or marker. This marker is *power*. The first stanza in effect describes this power, then bounces off it, as a referent, to introduce the second stanza and another kind of power, one that tortures animals for enjoyment.

Using our metatext, we are aware that frogs may be sources of water and that survival may necessitate their cutting open, but not for enjoyment. This cruelty is opposed to the right kind of power, compassionate establishments based on love. The *establishment* is often equated with the oppressive system of government, at least seen as oppressive by the Aborigines, and the first four lines of the second stanza is a plea for a transformation of this *establishment* into one based on love, but this is followed by a reiteration of the sadistic pleasures of the establishment based on its own kind of spirituality, or power, though even here the referents hold oppositions which stress hope rather than despair. A heat sign is followed by a cooling sign, pain is digested, and the sickly sight of spirituality is eaten which refers back to the digested pain.

Many Aboriginal rituals and ceremonies are based around such ingesting and egesting, of the burning pain of the initiating firestick and the cooling waters falling, of being eaten by the serpent and of being vomited by the serpent, and thus by seeing the last lines in an overall structure of Aboriginality, we may discern that being ingested and then egested is a sign of rebirth.

Poetic discourse is the equivalence established between a word and a text, or between a text and another text, with text being taken in the widest sense of meaning anything and everything which may be read.

Thus I have been seeing Aboriginality as a metatext, or the matrix beneath Lionel Fogarty's poems by which they may be read, or by which a first or second reading may be transcended into a much deeper reading.

Thus in our reading, the third stanza may be seen as the end result of initiation, or the rebirthing process, which again, according to the metatext of Aboriginality must be positive and natural. The sound signs scattered throughout the poem from *songs*, noises, and loud pains are transmuted into a barking laughter like running creeks; the falling water of the second stanza, and any negativity still remaining, dead weeds, dead seeds are seen as fecund with life-shining desire. A last line, *'Free our dreams'*, stands alone; and it is the dreams which are important, the source of power, a referent to the *Dreaming* of the Aborigine from whence comes all power.

By analysing this poem of Lionel's, I have attempted to show that it has a complex structure which necessitates some knowledge of the underlying metatext of Aboriginality. A supposition which I have made is that his five volumes of poetry may be taken together as a text, that they operate as a larger whole, or field in which the poems serve almost as chapters. Perhaps these single texts may be compared to the artefacts discovered in an archaeological excavation with the five volumes being the earth and the metatext being the culture which left those artefacts to be covered by the earth. Also I stress that the act of reading is unstable, and any interpretation is never final. Lionel's versions of these poems by being published have become fixed. They cannot be corrected, or amended, and any consequent rewriting will have them as a referent. They will remain in this form as will the ungrammaticalities of the texts.

These ungrammaticalities are important in that they threaten language as representation. The reader, especially the white reader will continually seek relief by escaping back to a safe reality where grammar is standardised and the only Aboriginal words met with are the place names of towns, suburbs and streets. But if Lionel Fogarty's poems are to be properly read, one must leave the safety of standardised language and place-words and plunge into an

Aboriginality which will reveal itself in a blaze of revelation, or a smile of understanding, though this revelation or sudden leap towards understanding is always chancy and is a never ending progress, since each re-reading forces the reader to once again check his or her interpretation. Lionel Fogarty's poetry is great poetry because we are forced to read and re-read it, and each re-reading yields us a little more of its substance. It is this which makes his work fascinating.

5

Listening to
the Fringe

THE POLICY OF ASSIMILATION WAS A WEAPON AIMED AT all aspects of Aboriginal culture, and secular song-making and singing did not escape attack. In areas where few settlers held large tracts of country, Aborigines could retain important portions of their culture, and even continue to be creatively active in producing original works in language and dance, but as time went by and Anglo-Celtic culture began to be spread by a communications technology of dominance, secular Aboriginal songmaking and singing began to decay. In remote areas such as the Kimberley, older people might continue to compose songs using Aboriginal verse structures such as the tyabi, but the younger people—especially those working on the large cattle stations or living as fringe dwellers around the towns—began to turn an ear towards new sounds

From the first contact with the invaders, Aboriginal songmakers had begun modifying their songs. English words were included, or the structure changed, for example a second stanza was added to the traditional single one. Examples of such modifications may be found in the Australian Institute of Aboriginal Studies volume by Luise A. Hercus, *The Languages of Victoria: a Late Survey* (1969, part 1, pp. 91–117). Eventually, and especially in areas where the local language was decaying or being replaced by a dialect of English, Aboriginal song types were replaced by

Christian hymns and nineteenth century dance music. Of notable interest was the gum leaf band. Christian missions introduced choirs and even decorous dance music as part of their attempts to assimilate Aborigines into 'civilised' norms. With the advent of the radio and motion pictures, simple diatonic tone structures were learnt.

A feature of the rural scene in Australia was the nomadic shows travelling from town to town. These were usually headed by a cowboy, western, or hillbilly singer of renown, for example Buddy Williams and Tex Morton who had gained popularity from their radio programs. These shows featured such acts as buckjumping, stockwhip cracking and rifle shooting—acts which appealed to the Aborigines, many of whom were engaged, or had relatives working in the cattle industry. There was a similarity between their lives and that of the American cowboy—both were itinerant agricultural workers—but through film and song the life-style of the American cattle worker had been glamourised. An Aboriginal stock worker without any power or glamour or dignity often found personal worth by identifying with these American cultural heroes. There was little or no identification with the indigenous American people often depicted alongside these white heroes. These films and songs were so structured and the position of the American Indian so like that of the Aborigine that any identification was precluded.

The dominant structure of the discourse, the way of telling the story, was ordered to glamourise Anglo-Celts. Using simple action plots, the western film became popular with the young stockmen dressed similarly in widebrimmed hats and boots. They took as role models nomadic heroes portrayed by Gary Cooper and other American actors. Along with the western film came cowboy songs sung by singers such as Gene Autry and Roy Rogers. These became song models in the rural districts not only for Aboriginal singers, but for white singers such as Slim Dusty. These white singers spread the song form, partially Australianised, throughout the country. From such travelling singers, Aborigines discovered the guitar. It had many advantages, being portable, relatively cheap, and easy to play in the simple major four chord strum used by these popular singers.

Country and western songs replaced Aboriginal song structures almost completely. The subject matter of these songs reflected the new Aboriginal lifestyles: horses and cattle, drinking, gambling, the outsider as hero, a nomadic existence, country-orientation, wronged love, fighting and the whole gamut of an itinerant life romanticised in the stockman/cowboy ideogram. Some Aborigines creating in this genre used it for social protest. One such song, 'My Brown Skin Baby', by Bob Randall, protesting at the forced removal of children from their parents has remained popular among Aborigines to this day being quoted in books, plays and films. Other songs by singers such as Herbie Laughton reflect the basic sentimentality of the genre. His 'Alice Springs Waltz' owes much to the long popular 'Tennessee Waltz'. The Central Australian Aboriginal Media Association (CAAMA) in Alice Springs has issued a number of audio cassettes featuring this song genre.

After the Second World War, Aborigines began moving into the cities and into an urban lifestyle in which these songs had little value, though country songs remained popular among the immigrants. Bands, among them Harry Williams and the Country Outcasts from Melbourne continued to play and record this music, but young city bands, such as Us Mob, sought new models in American popular song types. These were heard constantly over the radio and later television. In the sixties in all major cities traditional Aboriginal song structures were a thing of the past and were sung only by old relations visiting from the country. To many Aboriginal people, country and western was traditional Aboriginal music.

In the mid-seventies black music song types began to have some impact. One such music was reggae from the Caribbean, specifically Jamaica. This music with its lyrics purporting an identification with oppressed people, portraying itself as being sung by and directed at black people, and condemning European cultural influences on black people, appealed to young people attempting to rediscover their roots not only in an urban environment, but in towns like Broome and Alice Springs.

One of the most successful and popular Aboriginal bands,

No Fixed Address, saw themselves essentially as a reggae band, and could declare at one time that reggae was Aboriginal music. This compliment was returned in full in the volume, *Reggae International*, which describes itself as: 'The Sourcebook—definitive text', and which writes about No Fixed Address in these glowing words:

> In Sydney, New South Wales, Australia, there's an incredibly vibrant reggae band staffed by black people who used to be called aborigines. No Fixed Address is the group's name, and the music they make is extremely hard, Jamaican-sounding reggae, played so right and tight that pandemonium sometimes attends their gigs. 'Black Man's Rights', 'Greenhouse Holiday' and 'The Vision' are songs so full of reggae authority that they wouldn't be out of place on a Wailers or Culture album.

A strength as well as a weakness of reggae is that often it sings an ideology based on a back-to-Africa theology complete with an African God-King. Few Aborigines were prepared to accept such an ideology—though an article on the Rastafarians, the religious sect which at one time more or less dominated the music, did appear in the last issue of the Aboriginal periodical, *Identity* (Vol. 5, 1982). But the emphasis on an African Christianity was countered by a strong political line which stressed the underdog, racial black pride, and the adoption of an ideology of struggle. Although the music of Bob Marley became popular, most other exponents of the music did not. They did not enter the mass music market and so were not heard over the radio. Few young Aboriginal musicians were able to afford records or the equipment to play them. The music which influenced them came directly from the radio. This was either country and western or rock'n'roll.

In the mid-eighties with the growth of community radio stations came Aboriginal radio programs. Not only this, but the Central Australian Aboriginal Media Association began to record Aboriginal musicians. Already in 1972, a Centre for Aboriginal Studies in Music (CASM) was established in Adelaide, the capital of South Australia. The purpose of CASM was to meet the needs of urban Aborigines and to help the youth to overcome the effects of the fringe position they continued to occupy in the cities. CASM defined these problems as:

(a) Limited involvement in secondary education
(b) Limited skill training as a result of . . .
(c) Feelings of inadequacy (both personal and social)
(d) Limited opportunities for experiencing either personal or social 'success' in a chosen field of endeavour
(e) Limited opportunities to work together in a project which is both meaningful to Aborigines and accessible to the majority population.

Music, it was felt, owing to its central place in both traditional and contemporary Aboriginal lifestyles could be of value in helping to overcome these 'limitations'.

A course was established of social worth which brought together both traditional and contemporary Aboriginal music. It was thought that they might fertilise each other, develop side by side, or merge into one music of Aboriginality. CASM's course was divided into two sections, rural and urban, or traditional and contemporary.

The rural section aimed to:

(a) Develop tribal people's interest in their own rapidly disintegrating traditions by recognising the full authority and knowledge of tribal elders
(b) Use traditional Aboriginal musicians instead of white academics when teaching Aboriginal music
(c) Encourage traditional educational institutions to recognise traditional Aboriginal musicians as authorities in their own music.

The urban section aimed to:

(a) Teach and use music as one of the pillars of cultural identity and as a means of bridging the gap between black and white communities
(b) Aid the formation of bands and provide them with the

means of generating income and incentive to purchase their own instruments and equipment
(c) Create work opportunities by setting up regular venues and touring circuits
(d) Provide access to recording facilities and learning experience as a stimulus to the development of original composition, and the eventual establishment of a record label and distribution network oriented towards original songs that relate to old and new Aboriginal experiences
(e) Provide facilities for those musicians who are motivated by their opportunities to become music ally literate and wish to gain a more solid understanding of musical theory as well as techniques
(f) Set up a part-time teaching programme where advanced students from the CASM could give music lessons to Aboriginal people in Adelaide and music workshops in country towns.

CASM's program was similar to other music associations, such as Abmusic in Perth. It stressed that music had a social role as well as being entertainment. This attitude is close to that taken by The Aboriginal Writers' Oral Literature and Dramatists Association (AWOLDA) at their second conference in which one of the resolutions called not only for maximum independence for Aboriginal creative works, but also that they should have social value. There is a connection between Aboriginal writers and musicians in that Aboriginal poets have had some of their poems recorded by Aboriginal musicians. Aboriginal poetry with its regular metre is easily adapted to music. Again, Aboriginal poetry often is created to be heard rather than read and this means many poems are suitable as song texts. Oodgeroo Noonuccal has had several of her poems recorded, the most successful being 'No More Boomerang'. It has been recorded several times, the latest being by the Alice Springs based band Coloured Stone on their second album, *Island of Greed.*

CASM was successful in helping Aboriginal music to achieve a higher quality of musicianship and recording. In their course they also introduced young and up-and-coming Aboriginal musicians to other music such as reggae. They trained Aboriginal musicians who went on to form bands such as No Fixed Address and Coloured Stone in South Australia and Kuckles in Western Australia. Bands whose records and tapes are still very popular. CASM students from an urban lifestyle were able to come into contact with traditional Aboriginal music and musicians. This contact was so successful that many Aboriginal bands began using traditional Aboriginal instruments, such as the didgeridoo and clapsticks. Instruments which up until then were heard only in remote country areas, or on anthropological field recordings.

Although CASM did not fulfil all its aims, some of these have been carried out by the Central Australian Aboriginal Media Association (CAAMA) which has expanded into running a radio and television network. Apart from providing media access they have furthered Aboriginal music by setting up their own recording studio, Impartja, which has produced cassette collections of songs in both English and Aboriginal languages. These perhaps reveal the precarious state of traditional Aboriginal song, in that none of them feature traditional singers. Essentially their cassettes feature Euro-Australian forms from hymnal, through country and rock, to the more polished reggae and Black American-influenced music.

From this brief examination of CASM and CAAMA, it may be seen that contemporary Aboriginal music is in a healthy condition, though this cannot be said for traditional music. In fact on a secular level Euro-American song types have all but replaced those of a purely Aboriginal tradition. Because of this, it is important to consider how much of this music portrays a sense of Aboriginality, rather than just being a reflection of the prevailing musical trends in the majority culture.

Dr Hugh Webb of Murdoch University, Perth, has developed the concept of 'Ideotones', which he finds useful in studying contemporary popular music. These, he sees as audio-narrative units which flow from the music to suggest certain inevitable conjunctions that occur in the word/music nexus. They affirm or challenge the apparent unity of the dominant ideological discourses playing at any one time.

I'll give an example in order to make this clear. The Western Australian Aboriginal singer Josie Boyle recorded two songs 'Oh What A Day' and 'I Love Western Australia' — both in a breezy singalong mode which effectively affirmed Western Australian regional chauvinism. They also reinforced the forces of regionalism which are of a particular ideological concern in Western Australia. The state is isolated from the rest of Australia and this isolation has bred a strong regional identity. Her simple seeming songs ideologically affirm and accept in both word and tone, i.e. ideotone, the political and social situation in Western Australia.

In fact we could go on by using the concept of ideotones to reflect on the political position she occupies in Aboriginal affairs, although without knowing her other work it would be impossible to conceive of the degree of Aboriginality she projects. In fact her regionalism is tempered with a strong sense of Aboriginality, which has extended to forming a dance and song group. She is fluent in her language and has recorded a tape in Wongi a Western Desert dialect, her mother tongue. These are translations of American country and western songs This is her favorite genre, or type of song. The singing of this song type, a type often reflecting an ideotone of conservatism as well as an assumed radicalism of the 'rebel' or 'outsider' may be in itself sufficient to explain how Josie Boyle can write a song glorifying the winning of a yacht race by a millionaire, while being aware of so many Aborigines unemployed, so many rotting in jails and prisons, so many living in substandard housing and so on and so forth. Other Western Australian Aboriginal bands, such as Kuckles from Broome sing of the dark side of Josie's paradise.

Using Dr Hugh Webb's theory of ideotones, I am going to analyse two songs based on an Aboriginal hero of the Kimberleys The first is by the popular Anglo-Celtic 'folk' singer, Ted Egan, while the other was written and produced by Mark Bin Bakar, Coordinator of Abmusic, Perth. It is sung by Lucy Cox, a young singer from Broome. My first cassette is titled:

Ted Egan   The
presents   Kimberley

Even at first glance, I am aware that Ted Egan is as important as the Kimberley. The lettering of his name is of the same size, and 'presents' is lost in the background of the cassette cover illustration, which is of a Japanese pearl diver posed formally with his helmet on his knee. In small letters almost impossible to read are the musicians accompanying Ted Egan. What I receive in my reading of the cover is Ted Egan The Kimberley. This amounts almost to an identification. He is affirming that he knows what he is singing about, that he and the Kimberley are one, and this strong reading is maintained even if I reintroduce the 'presents'.

On the inside of the cover we find that the musicians featured are reasonably well known in folk music circles, and that the well-known writer, Mary Durack, MBE, recites one of her poems: 'Lament for the Drowned Country.' Thus from my reading of the signs I am led to believe that this tape is an authentic account of the Kimberley region. In reading the song titles I note that the first track is (what else?) traditional Aboriginal music. Other objective facts bear out the authenticity. One is that Ted Egan produced the tape thus keeping artistic control, at the expense of widespread distribution, though perhaps his recording company (RCA) did not consider it commercial enough for release.

I found my copy in Broome in the Kimberley, and the man I bought it from was loud in its praises. I later learnt that Ted Egan constantly tours country areas and has produced a number of regional tapes which he sells after his shows. He is thus his own distributor—and as he has visited the areas he sings about more than once, his tapes are evidence of his earlier visits during which he collected the material for the subsequent audio recording. Moreover, his regional recordings are testimonies not only to his authenticity, but to his continuing interest in these regions. In playing the cassette I found that the quality was excellent having none of that homemade roughness associated with small time recording producers.

My second tape has all the rough qualities found in a low budget production. There is none of the slickness of Ted Egan and the cover has obviously been photocopied. But this cover does reflect back on the singularity of the Egan cover. Ted Egan . . . The Kimberley . . . buttressed up with the single posed image of the pearl diver. In contrast at the top of this cover is scrawled:

KIMBERLEY LEGEND

and at the bottom:

LUCY COX

The space in between the title and the singer, separated as much as possible, is occupied by what appears to be a rock painting. This is scattered over in rock-painting style with Aboriginal symbols, weapons, hand stencils, a female mimi, Wandjina deity figures, and in the centre of the painting a finely etched image of a pearl lugger, though this does not dominate the cover.

We have pictured here the Aboriginal version of the Kimberley which is vastly different from the singular cover of Ted Egan's cassette. We would expect the songs to be different too. They are, and in this cassette there is little of the pretentiousness of a 'folk' singer of renown. There is none of that seeking to define a country by its materialist history made up of working class heroes and other 'folky' stereotypes, nor is there any Aboriginal traditional music at the beginning.

For Lucy that music is no longer relevant. Her music is contemporary Aboriginal and she sings in a light popular style about love, though in some songs touching on race, religion and history. There is no sweep of history, or the seal of man on the Kimberley as we find on the Egan tape. But the reason why I have selected these tapes is that there is a song on each dealing with the same historical person: the Aboriginal fighter, Tjandamara. Using Hugh Webb's theory of ideotones I wish to compare and contrast the treatment of the Aboriginal hero by these two singers.

In terms of ideotone identification, the songs may be

placed in genre blocks. Ted Egan is considered a 'folk' singer and his music may be placed in the genre of Folk Music (Australian). Lucy Cox sings a type of popular music with lots of harmony and soft electric guitar work. I shall shorten the genre classification markers to 'folk' and 'Pop':

IDEOTONES

Folk	Pop
Authoritative and authentic didgeridoo and clapsticks.	Strong bass guitar, drums sometimes sounding like clapsticks.
Story-sequence narration leading into the song. Voice recorded above instruments, standing individual and alone. White Australian voice, with rural gruffness.	Aboriginal voice, sometimes falling into the distinctive accents of Kriol.
Tone: assertive. Confident voice of the insider.	Tone: non-assertive. Flat style of delivery.
The folksinger with liberal views. A white voice calling for fairplay.	Statement of fact. Acceptance of Tjandamara.
Aboriginal rhythms, very authentic.	The sound of the wind, reggae-influenced rhythm echoing song title.
Images of history, sequential narration, call for a re-interpretation of historical facts.	Identification of ancestral male, Pidgin, with present generation.
Non-commitment. The past is dead.	Pidgin exists in mythical time, always present. We must accept his deeds and not feel at fault for doing so.
Questions? Was he a murderer, or a Che Guevara?	Answers. A freedom fighter who fought for his land.
Use of dominant discourse, and language selection reinforces the idea that he was a murderer.	Statement of fact. This is what he was.

The basic idea behind both songs is to narrate the story of Pidgin, the Aboriginal fighter in the Kimberley. Ted Egan's ideological stance is to reinterpret history, or rather to seek for a reinterpretation from his Kimberley audience. He reinforces his song text with an authenticity seeking to be Aboriginal. This is seen in the use of Aboriginal musical instruments. His approach is non-poetical, straight historical narration broken by a chorus or refrain.

Mark Bin Bakar, the composer of the Aboriginal song, and the singer, Lucy Cox, approach the life of Pidgin from a different perspective. It is poetic or mythopoeic, history is discarded in favour of an identification with the fighter, who is urged to fly away and be free. There is an opposition between white history and mythology, or even historical being and freedom. There is no question of historical reinterpretation, and none of the ambiguity of Egan. For Lucy Cox this has already been done, and she stresses that this is how it was. All Aborigines should cast away any shame at his methods and be proud of this Aboriginal man who by his actions has passed into legend.

I am presented with a white version and a black version, which I read as follows. Ted Egan as a white man identifying with the pioneers of the Kimberley feels unable to alienate his conservative audience by making a definite statement. Tjandamara/Pidgin after all was a black man who fought not only against the whites in the Kimberley, but in an ideological sense against the whole tradition of the pioneers and their heroic opening up of a new country. A tradition which Australian folklore glorifies at the expense of the Aborigine.

Thus although Ted Egan doesn't fully comprehend the ideological implications in calling for a historical reinterpretation (or does he?), I know that this calls also for a re-examination of his own role in the glorification of settlers who brutally decimated the local Aboriginal population and murdered those who stood against them. His questions therefore receive no worthwhile answers, and he even, in an ideological shift, transfers the eventual murder of Pidgin on to the Aborigines. He was betrayed by them. Thus the settlers are let off and need feel no guilt.

Ted Egan bases his appeal on history, and for him history is a folk history filled with wild and woolly characters who were taming a wild country. This too is history as myth—a white mythology seeking to evade any acknowledgement of historical injustice. What happened is past, though the legend might live on with any decision being decided in the framework of Che Guevara, Robin Hood, or Ned Kelly— all white heroes—and who will decide this but the mythical people unspecified in future. There is no acknowledgement that the issue has been decided already by the Aborigines, but then for Ted Egan perhaps Aboriginal people are not part of 'the people'.

As it is impossible to include an audio of the two songs, I end this chapter with the song texts.

FLY AWAY PIDGIN
(MUSIC: synthesiser, bass guitar, guitars, drums.)

Fly, fly away Pidgin,
Fly, fly away and be free;
Fly, fly away Pidgin,
Fly, fly and be free.

I dedicate this song to a man of my race,
Turn the pages, back to a Kimberley place.
They call him Pidgin, why?—no body knows,
His real name was Tjandamara, so the story goes.

Fly, fly away Pidgin,
Fly, fly and be free;
Fly, fly away Pidgin,
Fly, fly away and be free.

He fought for his people, he fought for their rights;
He fought for their freedom, and he stood up to fight;
He was sent to capture, a man of his own race,
He found fifty, he felt the disgrace.

Fly, fly away Pidgin,
Fly, fly and be free;

Fly, fly away Pidgin,
Fly, fly and be free.

They shot him dead, in a Kimberley cave;
His spirit lives on, so I singim my song;
They standard subjects, and we're part of it;
We carry no burden—no burden of shame.

Fly, fly away Pidgin,
Fly, fly and be free;
Fly, fly away Pidgin,
Fly, fly and be free.

TJANDAMARA

(Spoken) The white settlers called him Pigeon, the outlaw.
His proper name was Tjandamara. The former police tracker
became convinced that he should take up arms against the
whites who were taking over control of the land previously
occupied on an unfettered basis by the Aboriginal tribes.
During the years 1894 to 1897, Tjandamara and his followers
raided, killed and plundered. How will history judge him:
callous killer, or freedom fighter?

(Didgeridoo and clapsticks begin for song verses.)

In April 1897, Australia's whites rejoiced,
For the telegram came to say that he was dead.
The famous Kimberley outlaw betrayed and shot at last,
And as proof the police paraded his severed head.
The whiteman called him Pigeon, but none quite knows why,
Certainly he had a great ability to fly,
But his proper name was Tjandamara,
Honourable man of the Djeriya dreaming,
Born and raised in the Kimberley,
A hunter through and through.

(Chorus) So what do you say about Tjandamara?
What do you think of Che Guevara?
Were they justified?

And have they really died?
What's your opinion of Robin Hood?
Could you really call Ned Kelly good?
Are you satisfied, when you speak with pride?
Were they freedom fighters, or agitators,
Bloody killers, or liberators? —
Jokes aside.

It's the people who make the legends,
So let it be cut and dried,
What's the verdict on Tjandamara? —
The people will decide.

He once was a famous tracker,
For the Kimberley police,
He was sent one time to capture a man,
A member of his own race;
But the old man told the tracker
'It's time to make a stand,
Don't be a whiteman's puppy dog,
Drive the foreigners from your land.'

So he stole the whiteman's weapons,
Shot the police on sight,
Freed their chained up prisoners
In the middle of the night.
He formed a gang of fighters,
And he gave each man a gun,
And Tjandamara the tracker,
Became an outlaw on the run.

The police poured reinforcements,
And trackers by the score,
For three hard years they chased him,
While he taught them tricks galore.
He tricked the trackers, stole their rifles,
Tunnelled his way through stone,
Until at last he was betrayed
And trapped in a cave alone.

There in a place called Tunnel Creek,
He fired his final shot,
And one of his own race killed him,
The ultimate tragic blot.
They took his head in a bag to Derby,
Evidence for the court,
The end of Tjandamara,
Or that is what they thought.

(Chorus) So what do you say of Tjandamara?
What do you think of Che Guevara?
Were they justified?
And have they really died?
What's your opinion of Robin Hood?
Could you really call Ned Kelly good?
Are you satisfied when you speak with pride?
Were they freedom fighters, or agitators,
Bloody killers, or liberators? —
Jokes aside.

It's the people who make the legends,
So let it be cut and dried,
What's the verdict on Tjandamara? —
The people will decide.
The people will decide.

6

Framing the Fringe

THE VOLUMES OF VERSE, *WE ARE GOING* (1964), by Oodgeroo Noonuccal (Kath Walker) and *The First Born* (1970), by Jack Davis have similar covers. Oodgeroo laughs sideways, her white teeth challenging the whiteness of her beads. Her hair is neatly arranged and we may be sure that if we could see the rest of her it also would be as neat as a pin — the proponents of assimilation loved to use platitudes when dealing with the Aboriginal race. Jack Davis on the other hand gazes into the distance. His hair is short and his clothing is casual. Assimilation did not cater for bourgeois blacks. Worker, stockman, perhaps an odd-looking missionary boy, this was all a black man could hope to be in Western Australia, and in Queensland a black woman might become a domestic, as did Oodgeroo. She escaped from this by joining the army during the Second World War. She became a switchboard operator.

Both the volumes have prefaces. In Jack Davis' book, this is titled: 'Introducing the Author' — though as this is a book of verse, perhaps it should read 'Introducing the Poet'? It has been taken from a tape-recording made by Jack Davis in an interview with Richard Beilby, who, we learn from the flyleaf, is a novelist. On a first reading, it is apparent that the transcript has been cleaned up to remove any signs of true 'orality' such as false starts, sudden switches in subjects, use of pause markers and so on. Instead we have what may be described as a narrative discourse in the first person, and though there may be occasional deviations hinting towards the tape, scraps thrown to verisimilitude such as the use of contractions, there is little feeling of spontaneity. Perhaps the heading, 'Introducing the Author', was correct after all.

The foreword to Oodgeroo's book is written by James Devaney. He is identified in her next volume of poetry, *The Dawn Is At Hand* (1966) in which she writes the foreword. He is her good friend and critic who has taught her much. This foreword, in comparison to that of Jack Davis, is quite short and may form the basis of a comparison between the textual reconstruction of the two lives.

James Devaney begins with the obligatory 'first'. The first book of poems published by an Australian Aboriginal. Then her credentials are given, and these are not those of a poet. Oodgeroo at the time was:

Queensland State Secretary, Federal Council, Aboriginal Advancement League,
Hony Secretary, Queensland State Council, Advancement of Aborigines and Torres Strait Islanders,
Executive Member, Queensland Aboriginal Advancement League,
Member, Union of Australian Women,
Member, Realist Writers' Group and so on.

This is followed by a direct quotation from Oodgeroo:

'I am of the Noonuccal tribe of Stradbroke Island, near Brisbane, my totem the carpet snake. I was born in 1920 and arrived a week before expected, at the home of white friends where there was a wedding in progress; and the little black baby stole the show from the star performer, the bride. They named me Kathleen Jean Mary Ruska.'

Oodgeroo here is stating her Aboriginality, giving her tribe, her country, and totem. There is only one incongruous note, she is named by an anonymous 'they'. Who 'they' are is not stated, but it is significant that her names are strong Christian names, indicating that the little black baby is to be assimilated into the naming clan. She was to renounce this much later in 1988 and rename herself Oodgeroo in a final flinging off of assimilation. Grammatically, the 'they' can refer only to 'the white friends'. This is borne out by the rest of the foreword. The opening paragraphs of 'Introducing the Author' is in opposition to this. It begins with Jack Davis' father: William Davis, tribe not stated, reared by a white family until fifteen, itinerant station hand, but a good athlete. There is nothing of Aboriginality in this—only the government policy of assimilation which took by law Aboriginal children from their natural parents and placed them with white people. These facts are repeated again in a life story of Jack Davis, written in the first person but put together by Keith Chesson (1988). More details are given there, but in our text to the poems, the use of the sign 'family' can only refer to 'white family'. It is a sad fact that too many of us Nyoongahs have never known a 'natural' family.

The second paragraph is the female aspect of the male first. Jack's mother suffered the same fate as his father. She also was taken away from her black parents. The text then informs us that Jack Davis is part Aboriginal and his described life follows along the same lines as that of the father. He is assimilated and the text informs us that he was treated as white, though his writing is coupled with his working with full-blood people, and from a close reading I can conclude that his creativity belongs to his darker side. This might lead into an ideological discussion, for some Europeans have placed creativity as stemming from the more 'primitive' parts of a man's mind. I use 'man' here deliberately for in this theory the creativity of women is not considered. In fact women belong to that dark side of man's nature along with the so-called primitive peoples of this world.

In Oodgeroo's foreword, though written by a 'white friend', there is no separation between 'part' and 'full', although her life and forebears are similar to those of Jack Davis. These are treated, but only in two short paragraphs and are not as emphasised as in my comparison text. Her mixed racial origins are stated and dismissed in a short five

words ('Kath Walker is not a fullblood') as a full identification is assumed. She speaks on behalf of 'her people',
puts 'her race' first, is a dedicated worker for 'them', but
nevertheless believes in the common brotherhood of man.

On the other hand with Jack Davis there is a separation
between himself and his people. A result perhaps of that
disastrous early separation from his parents. He feels sorry
for the fullblood Aboriginal people and the conditions
under which they work, and even when he uses the possessive pronoun 'our' to modify Aboriginal people, it has the
tone of the white philanthropist, who sees an injustice and
sets out to remove it. It is only when he protests at the
curfew imposed on Aboriginal people and is jailed for
being the ringleader that an identification with his people
begins to show, but again it is a personal decision to become
involved in Aboriginal affairs. There is still that feeling of
separation from the Aboriginal people which is lacking in
our text on Oodgeroo.

The Jack Davis text, refurbished from a tape-recording,
reveals what it was like to be an Aborigine in Western
Australia and how the policy of assimilation was so successful amongst those taken away from their black parents and
handed over to whites, that they had a definite problem of
identification and suffered an estrangement from the Aboriginal community.

In effect, they became like the nameless character in my
novel *Wildcat Falling* (1965). Placed in an in-between land
of neither being white enough to be European or dark-
thinking enough to be an Aborigine, they suffered a trauma.
In our text this is hinted at when he, the author, says that he
suffered from nightmares when a child. Our text informs us
that these were the result of Jack Davis' sensitivity, though
this reason is brought into doubt by the statement that he
had his share of fights at school. The reason for these
fights? His non-acceptance by the white students. He was
called a 'nigger'. Then occurs a contradiction: '. . . so you
see all in all, we had quite a happy childhood. Race
relations never worried us.' It would be easy to accept this as
an ironical statement, except that the happiness of his

childhood is stressed through repetition and, moreover, it is this childhood which is given as the essence of his love of nature which permeates his poems, as well as providing an opposition between the freedom of the bush (childhood) and the enslavement of the city (adulthood). This idealising of childhood is a commmon trait in Aboriginal writing. It is difficult to account for it. Perhaps it is part of our selective reordering of our memories to suit the past we wish to carry with us, or adulthood—in comparison to childhood—is an awful state to be in? Whatever the reason, it is an ideological construct that we create to buttress our belief that we were happiest when a child. As adults, we hide (by forgetting) all our childish hurts, fears and slights so as to create a memory paradise in which we may shelter.

The happiness of childhood, or rather the fact of childhood is definitely an element in the subject matter and structure of Jack Davis' poetry. His poems are often childlike in their simplicity and present a natural quiet vision of the world. It would be easy to dismiss his poems as light, or occasional verses, except that he is an extremely capable writer. In fact their seeming simplicity hides the amount of work which has been put into them.

He favours well-worked rhymed verses often in quatrains revolving around a simple opposition. A particularly fine example of his work which has found a place in a number of anthologies is 'The First Born' which laments the position of his sad neglected race in opposition to a laughter and joy now lost. Perhaps it would be too deep a reading to push the analogy towards happy childhood and sad adulthood, but if we take into account the foreword to this volume, it would be easy to postulate it here as the primary opposition lying beneath the poem.

'The First Born' is framed in a series of questions asked by the land as mother to her dark race. We can see a child/adult entering here who once was happy, but is now sad. What has happened the mother asks again and again. The questions are left unanswered and the 'white' reader is left to supply answers.

Both Jack Davis and Oodgeroo have poems asking about the future of the Aboriginal people. Their questions and answers are culled from the sixties ideology taken from America called 'integration'. In *The First Born and Other Poems*, Jack Davis ends his volume with a poem called 'Integration', which is closer to Oodgeroo's, 'Assimilation-No!' Jack Davis calls for the worlds to combine, the door to be opened, the walls to be broken, separation to end, the peoples to stand together as one under the smile of God. It is precisely this that Oodgeroo is against. Wine poured into a flowing river is lost; oneness implies surrender and death, and so such assimilation into oneness is to be resisted. The Aboriginal people must keep their own identity, or else they are nothing. Her message is reinforced by oppositions and the image of the river is compared to the gum which cannot be trained into an oak, and there is a consciousness of keeping the past things which matter, and not joining into a oneness with a stronger other in which the Aboriginal people will end up as the losers.

Oodgeroo is the more political poet and her poems are well thought out protests which ring out problems and call for solutions, though sometimes on examination the slogan-like lines disappear from reason, and a poem like 'Aboriginal Charter of Rights' falls into a series of clichés. In her best poems, she names the enemy, and by so doing can rise above politics to sing of other things such as her son, or her country. Jack Davis, on the other hand, seems bound to themes and metres which constrict rather than release. In his latest volume, *John Pat and Other Poems* (1988), there is no advance in form.

I find that his second volume of poems, *Jagardoo* (1978) contains some of his strongest pieces. He appears to have passed through assimilation. His verses have become 'poems from Aboriginal Australia' and there is a sweet blackness in some of them which is not found in his earlier or later volume. The soft plaint of 'The First Born' has given way to the stronger verse of 'Urban Aboriginal':

> With murder, with rape, you marred their skin,
> But you cannot whiten their mind;

They will remain my children for ever,
The black and the beautiful kind.

Even the metred and rhymed verse takes on a new strength
of blackness in which the disciplined verse structure at last
begins to echo the chant of Aboriginal song cycles in which
no word is superfluous. 'Tribal Man in the City' is a fine
example of how rhyme and metre may be used:

> Black the night my mother bore me
> Black her pain to give me breath
> Black the wailing ever o'er me
> Black my tribal death.

This volume is illustrated by Harold Thomas, an Aboriginal artist from South Australia, and one of his drawings,
illustrating the poem 'Tribal Girl', is featured on the cover.
In traditional times, women were the peace offerings and
often they were sent ahead of the men as negotiators.
Women and children often feature on the covers of Aboriginal books. They are there to allay suspicion, to open a
dialogue into Aboriginal culture. But when I later come
across the same illustration in the text (p. 40), I notice that
it illustrates a love poem. A poem of forbidden love in that
the 'I' of the poem is in love with a woman who is
forbidden him by tribal law. The poem opens on a promising note of acceptance and love, but ends with a scream of
rejection:

> Gin, barefoot black gin,
> Keep your red earth and your wurley,
> I can walk my own path,
> In the sun or in the dark,
> And find my own affinity.

Again there is that tension of oppositions which structure
many of the poet's verses. A tension of rejection and acceptance, of Aboriginality and assimilation is at its most stress-
ful in many of the poems in *Jagardoo* (which is Jack Davis'
Aboriginal name).

The volume begins with ten poems depicting the joys of contemplating nature. In most of the imagery, I find not an Aboriginality of image but a Europeanisation of the Australian landscape as found in the poems of white poets. There are 'gossamer curtains', 'a coat of green', 'scarves and bonnets', 'weavers and dresses' all harking back to an industrialised age. None of the imagery is taken from Aboriginal culture, and it is only when we come to the next set of poems which are concerned with social protest that the images become crisp and Aboriginal. 'Freckled mind', 'akin to the colour of the belly of a dugite', and the beautiful line, 'she was born with sand in her mouth'. But then, the images waver. 'Ogres' and other images appear which a poet of Aboriginality should leave to the European writers of occasional verse. I enjoy some of Jack Davis' poetry, but on the whole, consider him a better dramatist than a poet.

Before leaving Jack Davis' *Jagardoo*, dedicated 'To all who fight for freedom's sake', I shall examine the foreword to this volume. This has been written by the Anglo-Celtic poet, Judith Wright. She is an eminent poet in her own right and it is a practice when introducing unknown poets to have some such famous person write a foreword as this will draw attention to the book, but Jack Davis at that time was not unknown. His first volume of poetry, published in 1970, had been reprinted the following year—a rare event in the poetry world. But then as I have written before, Aborigines are a fringe people; this is reflected in their literary works which must be stamped with the seal of approval by a white person, a missionary or anthropologist, or failing this a philanthropic person from the field of endeavour into which Jacky seeks to enter. It is a game which is slowly coming to an end, though forewords and afterwords continue to be written.

The first paragraph of the foreword establishes the place of the Aborigines in Australia. It also establishes Judith Wright's views on the subject as well as enabling her to distance herself from any guilt arising from the treatment of Aborigines. Thus a government on the other side of the world gives them the status of British subjects, and this allows the British and later Australian governments to take away not only their land, but their children. And so, it is the government who takes Jack Davis' parents away from their community. The objectivity of the style, a style aimed for by Anglo-Celtic writers, is almost transparent in its ideology: the blame is placed on an unfeeling government.

It is this objectivity which is praised in the verse of Jack Davis. Any emotion, any resentment, any anger, any hatred is to be seen objectively. It should never be seen as propaganda, as protest, but as springing directly from life's experience. Judith Wright requests us to read the poems thoughtfully, not because they are good poems, but because we owe a debt to the Aborigines which cannot be redeemed by any Budget allocations. Her argument is somewhat illogical and may be countered with: but what about the quality of the verse? We have to read through a number of paragraphs before we reach an answer.

Firstly, she declares that it is only recently that the Aborigines have found a voice, and this at a time when the last remnants of Aboriginal culture are being threatened by the incursion of mining companies on to Aboriginal land with the result that the dispossessed Aborigines are becoming fringe dwellers of towns and cities as reflected in the poem, 'Tribal Man In the City'. She goes on to write that perhaps the strongest feeling about Davis' poems is that of sadness, a sadness which manages to swamp any positive feelings of bitterness and violence. Judith Wright commends Davis for the wisdom to eschew this in his poetry and gives as an example the poem, 'Self'.

The first part of 'Self' is among the strongest verse Davis has written:

> Today,
> I will turn down
> The corners of my mouth,
> Erase my smile,
> Replace it with a frown
> Then see if it will own me.

Here Davis' taut mastery of the English language is evident, but in the second stanza the lines become longer and flabbier. The promise of the first stanza is left and there is a retreat into childhood, so safe and secure, as in the succeeding two poems, 'Balloons' and 'The Adventurer'. It is this second verse that Wright quotes as an example of Davis' wisdom, but I would say that his refusal to accept the latent violence within him has altered and transformed his poetry so that Judith Wright may describe many of his verses as simple appreciations of natural beauty too naive for a sophisticated audience and that they should not be taken on merit, but in the light of the poet's own gentle personality and background. This is the answer to the question I asked about the worth of his poetry.

I doubt if Jack Davis would agree with this summing up of his work, or even with the summing up of his personality. This text of Jack Davis leaves little to the imagination and results in the downplaying of his work. A reading of his poem texts does reveal flaws in his work, but if we accept assimilation as being responsible for these flaws, then we might approach such poetry with a deeper sense of trying to read what may not be written, rather than what is written. Assimilation has hindered Aboriginal creativity rather than helped it.

7

Assimilating a Fringe Identity

How do I read an old Aboriginal periodical like *Identity*? Published from 1972 to 1982, it has now assumed the status—or been devalued—of a historical icon, or artefact. It is no longer to be read as news, as a guide to what is happening on the fringe, as a medium of information about Aboriginal hopes and aspirations: hopes and aspirations filtered through the language of numbers of people who wished to communicate, who sent signs across the void to an editor who reproduced them into this magazine.

These signs were not only words. They included photographs and illustrations, cartoons and line drawings—all iconic representations towards recreating, or preserving, or keeping an Identity—though little thought went into exactly what this 'identity' was and how it should be expressed? The magazine had been cast into the shape of a conventional periodical and then floated on the world. It floated there for ten years, then submerged into the depths of libraries, strange fishes of Aboriginality drifting downwards to be hooked, not by the casual reader, but by the theoretician, by the academic, by the student. They come to ask, they come to at least glance, they come and there must be a question: what was this *Identity*?

Since the inception of *Identity*, questions have been asked by Aborigines and others involved in Aboriginal affairs, as to its purpose and ultimate objectives. To be precise in reply to such questions would, naturally, be difficult, considering the complexity of Aboriginal affairs, the direction such activities will probably take in the future, and the role Aboriginal people will perform, either as a group or as individuals, within the larger Australian society.

This was how Charles Perkins, later Secretary of the Department of Aboriginal Affairs, stated the problem in the editorial for the fourth issue in 1972. In my reading of his words, I find that he is advocating a political role for the journal and that there is an identification between Aboriginal affairs and *Identity*.

But in paragraph two of his editorial, his opinion is that the periodical should be an avenue of expression for Aboriginal people, 'particularly via the various forms of communication such as articles of fact, poetry, fiction and other art forms'. How am I to read this—in an ascending or descending scale of importance as to the means of expression? Obviously it is language oriented, and any other methods of communication are grouped under 'other art forms'. Perkins goes on to state that it is through such 'avenues' that Aborigines can identify as a group. This is vague; but I read it to mean that these 'avenues of expression' must be Aboriginal, that they must be signifiers of Aboriginality, or codes reifying group identity. Thus the periodicial is to have a political and social role.

This positive role for *Identity*, however, is watered down in his third paragraph, or rather the 'avenue' begins to narrow into a bush track. Now the magazine can 'perhaps play some small part', and 'perhaps help us'. All in all, the third paragraph indicates a lessening of the impact, a lessening of idealism, and this is carried into a fourth and final paragraph. The editorial finishes off on a note of pessimism:

'There is every reason to believe that *Identity* can make a worthwhile contribution to Aboriginal society and, in the long run, to the wider Australian society.'

I read an ambiguity in Charles Perkins' words which is reflected in the ambiguity of the publishing policy of the periodical. In seeking to cover the whole field of Aboriginal affairs, the focus drifts off true so that the periodical can be seen as a camera or instrument to be taken advantage of, rather than as an independent journal of opinion, or of the arts with a strong line of Aboriginality uninfluenced by varying degrees of assimilation unconsciously or consciously practised by some individuals.

Kevin Gilbert in the editorial to the previous issue, as a writer stresses that the periodicial is a vehicle of Aboriginality. He is aware that it is primarily a means of communication:

'that the policy . . . is that of presenting the cultural-social development of the Aboriginal people in a true and unbiased light and providing a forum for Aboriginal views and opinions of all kinds.'

It is important to note here that the methods of discourse are not touched on, that any policy on language is undisclosed, that it is assumed that the language is to be Standard English, and that the types of literature favoured are biased towards the social realist, in that cultural and social development are joined together in what appears to be a unity. Literature and the arts are seen to have a functional purpose and this is stressed by both Charles Perkins and Kevin Gilbert, with the latter calling on the readers to:

'Send us the myths and legends of your people; tell us of your achievements and experiences; describe how you live, whether on settlements or missions, as "fringe dwellers", or in cities and towns.'

The direction of the periodical was supposedly controlled by a managing committee of Aborigines, under a chairman, George Abdullah; but this direction owing to constant changes in committee membership, coupled with a lack of experience in framing an editorial line, was haphazard.

Constant changes meant that no continuing policy could be developed or adhered to, and the lack of experience meant that no decision could be taken on whether an Aboriginal means of communication be favoured or developed. The use of Standard English appears never to have been queried, or even discussed. It simply was accepted that the magazine would be in Standard English. This meant that many readers might accept that Aborigines had only one discourse available to them for communication. This was Standard English, the dominant discourse of the Anglo-Celtic Australian majority.

Jack Davis in 1985 in an unpublished interview with Marlene Chesson, then a student at Murdoch University, spoke about the problems he found when he became the editor of *Identity* in 1975. One of these was the weakness of the managing committee:

MC: Can you outline some of the controversies with the committees . . .?

JD: Oh yes, I can outline that because frankly, they didn't know what they were about. To a certain extent neither did I, at least I did have some expertise and some of the controversies were that they didn't know the difference between a noun and a verb and I did.

This lack of expertise which is often a feature of Aboriginal managing committees, means that their authority may be done away with, or transcended by a strong-willed committee member, chairman, or in this case editor. Jack Davis as a writer challenged the authority of the committee:

'If you're going to come in and tell me how to run this newspaper or how to run *Identity* and you don't know, then you better get yourself another editor.'

Thus during his time as editor, *Identity* followed the policies of the editor. Jack Davis saw the role of *Identity* as being essentially to get Aboriginal opinion across to white Australians. This meant in effect that the Aboriginality was diluted. It was not an Aboriginal magazine for the different communities, but a means to establish mutual understanding between the Aboriginal minority and the Anglo-Celtic majority:

> JD: It appealed to them to have Aboriginal people writing poetry, writing short stories and writing articles and that type of thing . . . I decided to keep it as conservative as I could.

This meant that any experimentation in language or mode of discourse was not considered. This is clearly stated in Marlene Chesson's interview with Jack Davis:

> MC: *How did you handle the Aboriginal people who didn't write* in proper English? *Some of the stuff that got sent down from the* Kimberley *for example?*
>
> JD: This was one thing which made the editor of Aboriginal Publications rather unique because I had to have those skills to be able to turn the stuff in — so it would be saleable and understandable to the buying public, and you must remember that we were trying to sell the magazine and make it a worthwhile publication. So anything that came to me that was not written clear enough for an English speaking audience, I had to use my skills to make the stuff readable, buyable, if there's such a word, and I did this by turning a lot of stuff — so it was readable for a buying public.

What this meant in practice was the editing out of much of the Aboriginality of style or discourse. This editing might be seen to have been against the basic aims of the periodical which had been stated in early editorials. One of these aims was to give a voice to Aborigines everywhere and to create a forum of pan-Aboriginality. This meant that a language policy should have been clearly worked out for the magazine. An opportunity was lost by not seeking to set parts of or even the whole magazine into an Aboriginal discourse, be it Aboriginal English or an Aboriginal language, or a mixture of the different discourse patterns spoken.

It may not be generally accepted, but the use of a language or a specific dialect is a political act. The use of Standard English by the first national Aboriginal periodical in effect meant that Aborigines accepted Standard English as the dominant discourse in Australia and the one to achieve, and to use. This was denying any Aboriginality of language and fostering an assimilationist policy. Still, for all the adherence to Standard English, *Identity* under the editorship of Jack Davis became extremely popular amongst Aborigines. They still remember the issues published during his years as editor and regret his leaving the periodical and its later demise.

Non-Aboriginality of language or mode of discourse was made up for by Aboriginality of content. Although it is impossible to reprint a whole issue for this book, it is of value to examine in detail a sample copy of this periodical which did help to get the Aboriginal message across to non-Aborigines, provide an outlet for Aboriginal writers, and with a nationwide circulation in the thousands strengthen pan-Aboriginality. Aborigines for the first time had their own magazine in which they were centred doing things for themselves, rather than having things done for them. In a sense owing to Aboriginal editorial control and the use of illustrations the dominant position of the written text was lessened, and occasionally could be ignored, though not forgotten.

For a close reading of *Identity*, or as it came to be called under the editorship of Jack Davis, *Aboriginal and Islander Identity*, I will use volume 3, number 6, April 1978 issue as a random example as it is close to hand. The first thing that I notice is the colour of the cover. It is a bright cerise, reflecting the bright colour of a Western Australian wild-flower. Most of the colours of the covers under Jack Davis were bright, and reflected the natural shadings of flowers, of land, of sky and so on. Apart from this the brightness of the cover called attention to the journal and also served to frame the brown skins of the people figured on it.

The illustrations on the front and back of this particular issue were of young children. In keeping with the symbolism of the cerise colour, the front illustration is a face in medium close-up of a young Aboriginal woman eating natural plant food. From the colour and style of her hair it is apparent that she is a member of a desert community and not an urban Aborigine. This is born out from the back cover illustration which is of two children in profile, but with different hair styles and dressed warmly. Their features and light-brownish hair colouring mark them as also members of a desert community, but on a trip to a city. This is borne out from the accompanying caption: 'Two little girls from the Western Desert'. The preposition 'from' recalls my attention to the warm clothing and to the understanding that they are on a trip to one of the colder southern centres of population, perhaps Perth.

As I study the illustration, I become aware that both of them are wearing hearing aids, and this reminds me of the high infant mortality in the Aboriginal communities and of how many children because of an early disease of the ear have been rendered deaf. It now becomes obvious why the editor selected this photograph and why the subjects have been placed in profile. It is not for aesthetic reasons, but to draw attention to the continuing health problems among Aboriginal children and that while the symptoms are treated the causes are not.

The theme of a group of young country people on a visit to a city is carried over into the illustration on the inside of the cover where two more girls are shown inserting a coin into a parking meter. The contrast is there to be read, from the front cover of a girl at home amongst the natural abundance of the bush and who is then taken to a city where even the space is rationed and must be paid for. Thus we have an opposition between the free bush and the unfree city. The cold 'alienness' of the city and of western culture which, although it does not remove the stresses imposed on the Aborigines by that culture, seeks to cure the symptoms by modern technology, the hearing aid, which like parking space must be paid for.

The periodical proper begins with a contents page in which only one of the authors of the listed articles is acknowledged—'Dave Sands', by Jack Horner. It is not stated who this Jack Horner is. Underneath the contents list in small letters are given the names of the staff of the Aboriginal Publications Foundation (APF) in this order:

J. Davis — Editor
L. Riley — Office Manageress
H. Munro — Telephonist/Receptionist
L. Forrest — Typist/Stenographer
R. Jones — Typist/Filing Clerk
B. Jackson — Illustrator
J. Cork — Machine & Camera Operator.

It is apparent that the staff is seen as a team, and that a community effort is involved in bringing out the magazine. This is borne out in many other issues where the staff is not even listed. This is different from other magazines where the editor is usually highlighted. At the bottom of the list are the words identifying the girl on the front cover as 'A Lass from the Western Desert'.

The right side of the page is headed with a very large COMMENT in bold black letters. This commands our attention to the publishers — The Aboriginal Publications Foundation and its role:

APF will in future act as a referral body to the Aboriginal Arts Board with the object:
   (a) To publish books, pamphlets and other publications by and for Aboriginal Australians.
   (b) To commission such works for publication.
   (c) To organise training for Aboriginal Australians in literary, visual and other relevant arts and crafts.
   (d) To provide scholarships, fellowships and advances and other assistance for Aboriginal creative artists of promise.
   (e) To conduct competitions, arrange exhibitions and in other ways recognise and reward distinguished performance by Aboriginal Australians in the literary, visual and related arts and crafts.

These objects appear laudable, until on a second reading I realise that the APF is only a referral body to what was then the Anglo-Celtic dominated Aboriginal Arts Board, which had the final say on the referral. It then becomes apparent why the word 'COMMENT' has been written in such large letters and the staff of the Aboriginal Publications Foundation in such small and insignificant type. The foundation was in effect a fringe organisation with little or no control over its finances or programs, and with a staff of seven, the majority of whom were office workers, it had little chance of formulating or planning anything beyond the quarterly issues of the periodical. It was another case of an Aboriginal organisation being relegated to the fringe with all decision making resting in other hands.

The first article is about the Cairns' Coral Hostel which is completely under the control of Aboriginal people and is a fine example of 'Aboriginalisation'. This is a familiar example of an article of how the Aborigines are advancing, but apart from this cliché, the words are illustrated with photos of staff and some of the students. These are valuable in that they may serve as historical records. It must not be forgotten that Aborigines are very conscious of their past, present and future as a collective whole and that what may be seen as ephemeral photographs illustrating only an article of local and present interest may crop up years later in another context.

An aim of *Identity* was to foster an identity amongst Aborigines and to strengthen group bonds, and such articles with accompanying photographs was a way of doing this. But a deeper reading of this laudable enterprise reveals that while 'the hostel has been a vessel which has conveyed scores of young Aboriginal and Islander people to a better education', this education is revealed as secretarial studies ('this has been . . . an invaluable supporting facility to their schooling in secretarial studies'). It is an important point which a first reading may fail to disclose and in fact refers me back to the Aboriginal Publications Foundation and its supporting role. The lack of expertise in this body was not in the secretarial field, but in the lack of skilled management staff who might be in a position to query the supporting role assigned to it. Lack of suitable higher qualifications has always been a noticeable lack in Aboriginal affairs, and such an invaluable support facility might have been used in helping to educate Aborigines into becoming managers of their own organisations.

As I have already written about the ideological problems implicit and explicit in the use of Standard English as the main vehicle of discourse in the periodical, it is of interest that the next article, written by Keith Chesson, is 'Language'. This acknowledges the importance of language as 'the medium through which a community transmits its world view', but the ensuing discussion is not extended to the role it has in such periodicals as *Identity*. It deals mainly with language within the Aboriginal community and language use between Aborigine and European in a historical context. It recognises the political role language plays within the Aboriginal community, but does not extend the argument to cover interracial relations and the effect this has on discourse.

The next article is 'Australia, New Zealand and Race Relations', by C. N. Perkins, and is about the inferior position not only Aboriginal people in Australia, but other indigenous people occupy in many countries. This position is put as 'Which way should we turn in order to survive, and then to develop?' The position of the Aborigines in Australia is then contrasted unfavourably with the Maoris in New Zealand, and the article ends with a note that fellowships are available for individual Aborigines to travel to New Zealand.

A problem encountered in a reading of such articles is that there is no indication of the community to which the writer belongs, especially as many Aborigines now have Anglo-Celtic names. Thus there is a problem of identity as to name. I even may assume that the article is by a sympathetic White, or that it is a government handout to publicise the availability of fellowships for travel and study tours in New Zealand. Apart from the problem of individual identity, the use of Standard English acts as a distancing mechanism in that we who speak and use it may find ourselves separating from Aboriginal communities for whom it is not a first language. We may begin to hear them as distinct entities in which we, as Aborigines, have little in common, especially if we live in cities and enjoy a standard of living on or near the level of the majority society. Thus, although we might regard ourselves as unassimilated, it is difficult for other Aborigines to accept this.

In reading this article, I notice that 'they' and 'I', the main subjective pronouns of the discourse, often are used to separate the Aboriginal people from the writer of the article. Even when *our* is used as a possessive pronoun in '*our*' effects, this still could be read as a collective pronoun used by a white person employed in the Department of Aboriginal Affairs—this fact being signified for me in a succeeding paragraph when the subject '*I*' accompanied the Minister for Aboriginal Affairs to New Zealand. This reading of separation between the writer and the Aboriginal community is reversed however at the end of the paragraph, in the sentence 'There is much we could learn from them'. Still, does this indicate that the person is an Aborigine? I may read ambiguity into it. Is it an Aborigine writing, or a public servant identifying fully with his job? This problem of 'identification', when Standard English is used and an Aboriginal readership is addressed, is ever present. In this book, it is both a problem and contradiction, even though I declare that I confront this problem in other of my writings.

The problem is often absent in oral discourse. Aborigines are usually fluent either in their language or in their Aboriginal English dialect and they use these in communication with other Aborigines. I bring this up as an example because if it is possible for us to do this in oral discourse, there is nothing to prevent us from so doing in our written discourse. In his article, 'The politics of Aboriginal literature' co-authored with Bruce McGuinness (1985, pp. 50-1), Denis Walker recognises that the use of white discourse styles serves to continue the process of dependency. He declares that the only way to change this is by turning to the discourse or speech patterns of the Aboriginal communities. This is an important point to consider especially when in writing we have an Aboriginal readership firmly in mind. This brings up the question of what readership I have in mind? It varies from the student to the general reader both White and Black who are at home in Standard English.

The next page (eight) contains two photographs of members of the National Aboriginal Congress. The top photograph is of the chairman and vice chairman (identification by caption), although the chairperson is a woman, and the bottom one is of the NAC members who attended a meeting in Canberra. This, in keeping with the composition and consultative role of the Congress, pictures the members with smiling faces. They have been scrubbed up to represent, or project an assimilated picture of smiling Aborigines with little or no contact with the conditions of the fringe camps. There is little conflict inherent in this photograph, though on closer examination, it is observed that the delegate from Elcho Island refuses to go along with the image. He stands with an unsmiling face and his hands are behind his back in contrast to the rest of the delegates whose hands are plainly in sight and empty. He appears on guard and wary in the city of Canberra and reflects the unease manifested before in the inside cover illustration of the two young girls from the Western Desert feeding a coin into the parking meter.

The next article has been taken from the Perth daily newspaper, the *West Australian,* and is entitled UTAH'S PROFITS. The letters are large and the text is accompanied by two illustrations which give the Aboriginal perspective — that the mining company Utah is making its record profits by wrecking the land. In the photos there is again an opposition: between technology and nature, or machine and land. The technology is foregrounded in both illustrations and the barrenness of the surrounding landscape is blamed on this technology. In the second photograph, a huge excavator is eating away at the land and leaving it bare, barren and utterly featureless. It is as if Utah is undoing the work of the creative ancestors who in the Dreaming marked out the land.

Page twelve draws attention to the fact that the Australian Institute of Aboriginal Studies has produced a map marking the boundaries of the different Aboriginal communities. The portion of the map reproduced is centred on Darwin, which is shown to be in Larakia country. There are no blank spaces of unknown terrain and the whole area has been parcelled out into tribal lands. Although it is not stated in the accompanying text, this signifies that Australia was not the trackless wilderness which the Europeans (Anglo-Celts) used as a pretext to occupy it.

A literary page follows the map. This is occupied by the prize winning poems from the Ronald and Catherine Berndt Prize for Poetry at Dhupuma College in Eastern Arnhem Land. The prize winning poem of Joyce Yikawidi is printed, as are the highly recommended poems by Ruthie Marrwulpul, Tony Wurramarrba and Albert Waninymarr. The first two poems are in free verse and are critical of the whiteman's role in destroying the land and Aboriginal culture. Ruthie's poem, 'My Life', flows in Standard English, but Tony's, 'I Can Still Think', although it may have been edited by his teachers, still retains an authenticity of Aboriginal expression and perhaps was originally written in Kriol and after edited closer to Standard English. The Aboriginal discourse style may be seen in such lines as: 'Blackmen know nothing of black-rock leave them/untouched . . .'

Albert's poem, 'After the Rains', is closer to a European model. It consists of four sets of triplets, with the first two lines rhyming, and the third line rhyming with the third line of the succeeding stanza. It appears a very accomplished piece of work. The prize-winning poem, 'Water Lilies', is a nature poem describing the growth of waterlilies in the waters of a river. It is Aboriginal in content and also in style as are the other poems in that metaphor and simile are not used. These occur seldom in traditional song poetry. Also there is no mention of the flowers of the waterlilies being beautiful, or any of the swooning approach bequeathed to European nature poetry by the Romantics. It is noticeable how the Aboriginality of the poem is stressed in that the waterlily is seen as a food source and not as a thing of beauty:

> Lilyroots stuck in the
> Hard dark mud

> Waiting for somebody
> To get them.
> They are big round
> Roots;
> Like peanuts.

'Peanuts' places the stress on the food value. With the exception of some of the verse of Jack Davis, Aboriginal poetry is not concerned with the overpowering beauty or intoxication of nature and land. There is an acceptance of both land and nature which appears foreign when contrasted to the poetry of white Australians. Also the primordial split between man and nature as found in European poetry and which is a referent to the dualism implicit in European thought, is absent. Any alienation is reserved for the immigrant culture and the ways of the immigrants. This is a signifier of Aboriginality in that oppositions are between culture (white)/nature (Aboriginal); cities (white)/country (Aboriginal); technology/land; and so on. The Aborigine is placed firmly in the landscape, or on the landscape and buildings and cities are intrusive elements into a pristine oneness, the loss of which is regretted.

Perhaps the one piece of modern technology which receives acceptance is the motor vehicle and this is seen in the cartoons of which there are a number in the periodical. It is noticeable that all of them are set in the bush and two of them concern motor cars driven by Aborigines. The first one is about a race between two men in a car and an emu in which nature is triumphant in the caption: 'They think they're fast, wait till I really move'. The second one is the last cartoon on a page titled Humour. It has been drawn by Ben Jackson. He depicts the car stalled on a flooded road. The cartoon does not involve the vehicle, but the flood which is the result of an evangelist praying for rain.

Under the editorship of Jack Davis, short stories were a strong feature of the periodical. Our issue features two of them. One of them, 'White Fantasy—Black Fact', is by the editor and is about individual black-white relations and how prejudice lurks in the righteous breast, though sometimes not in the unrighteous breast—in the story represented by a bikie gang who come through with flying 'colours'. This story would bear a deeper reading as beneath what appears to be a simple moral tale, there is quite a complex structure which may go back to European medieval moral tales, but I shall leave it to take up the second story, 'A Story of Wongawol Station' as told by Snowy Hill and transcribed by Anne Parker. This story is interesting in that it is a typical fringe story complete with a short editor's introduction, inviting us to read it in a certain way, in a realist way:

'It is useful to understand the real life situations as they occurred in order to get some feeling for the problems we have inherited today.'

Now when I am confronted by a text, once spoken but now wrenched from its social context, how do I approach it? As a piece of history, as a realist story detailing real events as they once happened? In this story there is nothing to indicate that the events are real, or if there is a frame of reality, that this has not been altered in the course of the storytelling. It must be borne in mind that language does not mirror reality and that by relating a story the reality always escapes. In essence what happens is that the reader establishes a new reality for each reading of the story, and in oral storytelling the narrator establishes a new reality for each audience.

It is the narrator, his voice and the audience which bear any reality, not the story itself which changes to fit the audience. Thus in oral storytelling there is never any fixed text, only a fluid narration which appears to be fixed by a metatext or structure residing in certain fixed traditional forms. This metatext, or structure may be discovered by the critical method termed 'structuralism'. If we use this method we may discover a traditional structure, or plotline determining the way the story is told. The plotline, or structure, is fixed and the words of a new story must be adapted to fit it.

Snowy Hill's story relates incidents which supposedly

occurred between his brother-in-law, Jimmy and his white boss, Tommy Mellon. I leave aside here the Aboriginal elements at the discourse level to concentrate on the structure of this narration of 'real' incidents. These fall into a pattern:

I Boss's Trick.

1. Tommy Mellon, although the boss, tricks Jimmy into collecting wood supposedly for the camp fire, but really to build up a supply to be used when mustering cattle. The lack of social equality between Tommy and Jimmy is shown in that he must follow orders.
2. He finally rebels and they fight. Rebellion.
3. Jimmy's wife saves him from being shot by his boss. Implied sexual motif.
4. She warns Jimmy to be careful. First warning.

II. Reversal of Trick: Jimmy's Trick.

1. Boss sends an unarmed Jimmy out with an armed man. Emphasis that the man will shoot Jimmy.
2. Jimmy uses the trick of collecting fruit, quandongs, to keep behind the man.
3. He saves himself.
4. Jimmy's wife warns him to be careful. Second warning.

III. Jimmy's Second Trick Fails.

1. Boss sends Jimmy out with a white man.
2. He kills a bangary (a goanna) and is beaten up.
3. He cures himself by using the Aboriginal method of smoking himself over a fire.
4. Tension between the two. Both decide to teach the other.
5. Jimmy tricks the white man into being off guard.
6. His trick appears to fail and they fight.
7. Jimmy wins and beats up the man and leaves him behind after taking his weapons.

IV. Jimmy's Third Trick.

1. He goes to Wiluna with the weapons.
2. On the way, he steals supplies from a shepherd's camp.
3. Supernatural element: Mapan (magician) element intrudes, a common element in these stories. He hears the shepherd's

comments from quite a long distance. He has outwitted, or
tricked them again.
4. He reaches Wiluna and informs on Mellon.

V. Second Trickster Reversal.
1. The policeman disguises himself as a prospector.
2. He takes notes.
3. Different offence intrudes. He sees who sleeps with the
white men. This refers back to the sexual motif.
4. The policeman goes away.
5. Mellon is outfoxed and hung in a chaff bag.

VI. Realist End Frame.
1. Absence of the hero or trickster, Jimmy.
2. All the Aborigines are sent away south.
3. Mellon loses his station.
4. End.

Now the folkloric 'trickster' character is found in many
cultures thoughout the world. These include the cultures I
am familiar with in Western Australia. I would like to say
here that I am not accepting the above story as a typical
trickster tale as may be found in traditional culture where
the 'trickster' is often a heroic type employing his tricks for
the good of his community, but as a modified story based on
the structure of the traditional trickster tale. It is this that
determines the story and its elements.

A folktale usually has a formulaic opening and an
atemporal introduction, like 'Once upon a time'. In our
story it is difficult to say if there was such an opening, in
that we do not know how the editing was done, or if the
story itself was embedded in a general conversation from
which it was extracted. In fact the story begins abruptly, as
if the editor had cut off the preceding dialogue. A temporal
introduction, such as 'When I was a boy' is also missing,
though at the end the temporality of the story is stressed. In
Aboriginal terms these missing signifiers mean that what is
called a 'true stori' is being related. A story constructed out
of the events which happened at a particular time and
place.

An oral narrative may be seen as a theory which sets out

the logical consequences which flow from the conjunction of two or more pairs of contrasts such as life/death, male/female and so on. These are oppositions which cannot be easily resolved by the community which suffers them. The folktale provides a method of interrelating and mediating dilemmas facing the community. In our tale the dilemma sought to be dealt with is black and white relations with all power being held by the latter. The problem is how can the power equation be equalised? The story tackles this problem and seeks to resolve it through traditional means. The traditional trickster, Jimmy, is employed to see if through trickery the power equation may be solved. The first point to be noted is that he must bring in a variable from outside the equation to do so. He brings in an outside force with disastrous consequences. The Aborigines are exiled away from their land.

A folktale performs its function by setting out an array of possibilities in a narrative form and usually deals with more than one set of oppositions which are dramatised through the actions of the characters, that is a number of equations are set to be solved. The various positive and negative states such as social harmony/social disharmony are conjoined by pairs into sets until all possible combinations are realised and a resolution given. It is then that the mediation process is complete, the equations solved and the story concluded. In Snowy's story this mediation process is set in motion and completion attempted by bringing in an outside force. An unknown variable, which instead of completing the mediation process renders it impossible. The result is disaster. The answer is plain: don't go this way!

By analysing the story in this fashion, I reach the conclusion that during the Depression when the events of the story supposedly occurred, no mediation was possible between the Aboriginal people and white people, and that traditional Aboriginal methods of oral narrative have a much deeper meaning than commonly supposed. In fact, if a structural analysis of collections of oral narratives such as *Gularabulu* (Roe, 1983) is done, we shall find a mediation process at work in the structure of the narratives. Such narratives are intellectual attempts at solving the Aboriginal predicament in post-Invasion Australia.

This discussion has led me some distance from my examination of *Identity*, though it is pertinent in that the contrasted opposites of European and Aboriginal lie at the heart of the structure of the periodical. This is reflected in the parts as well as the whole. Emphasis swings from Europeanised to Aboriginalised, and so after the Aboriginal story of Snowy Hill, there is a centrefold featuring Rosalyn Watson who has become assimilated into European culture as a ballet dancer. Ballet is a form of European high culture with little of the folk or popular arts in it, and any Aboriginal dancer would be well advised to reflect on the implied opposition between dancing on the points of one's toes and with the whole foot. In the periodical, in the last three photographs of the centrefold, dance is brought off its toes and flatfooted on to the earth by Aboriginal children being taught dance in an Aboriginal dance workshop.

The centrefold reveals the stress in the editorial policy under Jack Davis. This was an uneasy mating of Aboriginal and European elements which while it reflected the diversity of Aboriginal individuals also followed his aim of producing a conservative magazine appealing to as many people as possible. He was successful in his endeavour to explain at least some aspects of the fringe minority to the white centre.

Charles Perkins had developed an influential role in Aboriginal affairs. He was based in Canberra, the artificial Capital of Australia. He decided that the editorial office of *Identity* should be moved there. An immediate effect of the move from Perth was the resignation of Jack Davis as editor. A secondary effect was the snapping of the fringe link. The periodical became an adjunct of the educated Aboriginal elite assimilated into the central government bureaucracy. The fringe frame of photographs and covers was replaced with photographs of well assimilated Aborigines, or Aborigines at committee meetings. The cover illustration became a stylised logo, a dancing figure which could be confused with an African carving. Identification was not helped by the removal of Aboriginal and Islander from the title and a reversal back to the old single word name, *Identity*.

Under Jack Davis, community had been emphasised at the expense of individuals. Only rarely did the names of the editorial staff, or those of the Foundation Committee members appear. Often, even the names of the writers were not featured on the contents page. This changed in Canberra, though the magazine fell behind in its publishing schedule. The move to Canberra resulted in the continuity of the magazine being disrupted. The month printed on one issue had to be blacked out and then the month of issue was deleted. The periodical became an occasional publication. Even so, the producers of this occasional magazine are listed on the contents page under their respective titles: Editor, Writers, Printers, Publisher, Committee, Patron, Public Officer. All in all, it may be declared a more professional approach, though in the process, the fringe was forgotten. There was an emphasis on the pictorial arts and articles on political subjects with the only literature being a few poems. Short stories and legends were absent, and the English solidified into a Standard English edging towards journalese or bureaucratese. In 1982, the first national Aboriginal journal, *Identity*, ceased being published and passed into history. It is still missed by many.

8

Talking Fringe and Writing Fringe

PADDY ROE IS A STORYTELLER IN BROOME. HIS STORIES have been taped, transcribed and published under the title *Gularabulu* (1983) by Stephen Muecke. In his transcription, he used a new method of putting the stories into print. This, he claims, is a more authentic way of treating Aboriginal oral narratives as it seeks to preserve the way they are spoken. To show his method of transcription here is an example from the story 'Djaringalong' (p. 77):

That's Djaringalong—
Djaringalong you know he used to travel from there—
(Stephen: Yeah) he used to travel from there—
he come up here to pick up lil'—lil' fellas—
you know that's for his—
nest to feed his—
young ones—
he gotta get something for them to eat—
but he pick up—
babies from there—
Boy girl anyone babies—
when he pick these fellas up then he go back all
   time
   back here to his nes'—
feed all his—
young ones too—

> well, that time he didn't have any young ones yet,
>   really —
> that fella didn't have any ones yet he only had
>   two eggs —
> you know, he musta eat these himself too —
> every afternoon he go out —
> pick-em-up he come back again towards morning —

A problem with this method is that the story telling appears in my eyes to be fragmented. When I listen to the tape this fragmentation disappears and Paddy Roe emerges as an accomplished storyteller. This does not mean that I prefer the text rewritten to conform to Standard English. This same story, or a version, has been recorded from another Broome storyteller, Butcher Joe Nangan by Hugh Edwards who published it in a volume of Aboriginal stories called *Joe Nangan's Dreaming* (1976, p. 44). He rewrites the whole story. Here is the first paragraph of his published version:

> Long, long ago in the Dreaming days, in the far North, there lived a giant eagle named Djaringalong. She had a nest in the top of a Largardi, a Boab tree, near the sea, and the bottom of the tree was strewn with skulls and human bones — for the she-eagle lived on babies and small children that she snatched up in her long, hooked talons.

Immediately I am aware of the vast difference in discourse, or the way the story is told. The plotline, or succession of events are similar enough for me to identify two variants of the same story. I am aware that in oral forms of narration, there is never the same story told twice even by the same storyteller. It varies according to such things as audience, place, time and so on. This is different from a written story which has a fixed text directed at an imaginary 'general reader'. There is no contact between author and reader except through the written word, or text. In the oral process, the story telling is immediate, and communication passes directly from storyteller to listener. The storyteller can thus tailor his text to his audience and change it at will.

When I read the passage of 'Djaringalong' beginning the story of Paddy Roe, I am aware that he is addressing a particular audience, and is even stopping the narrative flow to emphasise and even elaborate on certain points to this audience—for example the problem of the eggs not being hatched and thus who ate the people? Also there is that 'yeah' from Stephen in brackets which helps me to identify the audience. With an Aboriginal, or local audience, there would not be the need for so much explanation as it is highly probable that they would know the plotline and could make the necessary connections. In my second example, where the orality has been edited out, the story has been changed into a written text from which the reader must get all his information.

I have given both these examples in order to show the extremes of transcribing or rendering Aboriginal oral stories into a written form. Two strategies have been adopted. The first, Stephen Muecke's, seeks to be as objective as possible and he appears to be a recorder of Aboriginal discourse. He gives us a transcript of the story and tells us in his introduction that this is faithful to the discourse of an Aboriginal storyteller. Hugh Edwards after recording rewrote the story completely. He does away with the Aboriginal discourse of Butcher Joe Nangan and becomes the narrator himself.

In the past, Anglo-Celtic recorders of Aboriginal oral stories or narratives rarely tried to remain true to Aboriginal discourse patterns in their written text. Usually, there was a complete abdication of any responsibility in seeking to be true to what was heard, in the sense of how it was heard. In fact, Kipling and others had created the form of the folktale which was in Standard English. Folktales were marketed as children's literature and thus were seen as an educational medium. The English had to be grammatically correct to provide models on how English must be written. Some collectors and writers (editors if you will) were aware that the spoken word was different from the written word, not only in regard to Aborigines, but also to the different social strata of their own society. This sometimes was acknowledged in forewords or introductions, but still there was the ready-made form of the folktale to fall back on. This, they considered, was a universal form into which all oral stories might be fitted without stress.

This attitude towards oral story telling passed over to the assimilated Aborigines. In the legends appearing in the periodical *Identity* there was an editing towards the fixed discourse of the Europeanised folktale, rather than towards the fluidity of fringe Aboriginal English. This is not to be wondered at, for Aborigines shaped by assimilation had read such folk tales and believed that their legends should not only have this form but be in Standard English. Aboriginal English was to be edited out; oral story telling was to be encased in the strait jacket of written Standard English, and Aboriginal stories and legends were to be standardised to take their place among the folktale collections of other cultures whose oral literature had suffered the same fate.

Fringe cultures are under constant pressure from the centre to conform to its dictates. These dictates are pushed by white researchers and educators on to Aboriginal people so that they learn to produce texts which in effect support the ideologies and mechanisms of oppression characteristic of conquest and colonisation.

Of course this may not be accepted. It may be stated that there is a discrepancy between orality and literacy, that oral communication works through immediacy, or spontaneity, whereas writing is planned, is organised and thought out. This is seen in our two examples. Joe Nangan's story is not the result of spontaneous thought, or even of any attempt at utilising the elements of spoken discourse, such as repetitions, and a direct addressing of the reader. In fact it appears that Joe gave a version of the story to Edwards who then questioned him on the salient points, removed any discrepancies in the succession of events making up the story, then produced a completely new text based on all the information gained. This is much like the reader reading a text, then plagiarising it. This is beyond the work of an editor, whose job is to 'correct' a text while keeping to the style of the original. After Hugh Edwards is through with the oral text of Joe Nangan, there is not much left of Joe Nangan's style. This is recognised by the writer in his foreword:

'Most of all I regret that Joe could not tell the stories himself in his own way.'

This means that there is little Aboriginality in the discourse, and any sense of Aboriginality is found only in the place names, illustrations, and the few Aboriginal words allowed to remain in the text. What is assumed by writers such as Edwards is that the devices utilised by spoken and written discourse are diametrically opposed, and that a direct transposition of the devices from one medium to another will not work, or even result in intelligible communication. Of course with the oral account of Djaringalong before me, I find that this is not so, and that a more honest editing of the Aboriginal text is possible.

The opposing of orality and literacy is often used when people compare the qualities of written and spoken texts. Stephen Muecke in *Gularabulu* confronts this problem in his foreword. He writes:

'The simple act of writing down stories (as well as phrasing them in good English) inevitably involves departures from Aboriginal narrative style.'

If oral texts must be transcribed and written down, then an audio cassette should be supplied along with the book; but if this is impossible, then the editing process utilised should leave the text as close to the original as possible. A third course might be to create a written style in close proximity to the oral style. I have tried to do this in my latest fictional work, *Doin Wildcat, A Novel Koori Script* (1988). This is written in non-Standard English, but without the repetitions and pauses of a true oral text. This has had a mixed reception amongst both Aborigines and Europeans. Some find it a joy to read; some difficult, and others unreadable.

The hegemony of Standard English in the different ex-British colonies has been challenged, but except for Pidgin in New Guinea rarely overthrown. There has always been an opposition between the 'broken English' of the various Kriols which have developed and Standard English. This has its counterpart in the political set-up where Standard

English is the language of the ruling elites, while the mass of the people speak Kriol. This is precisely the case in Australia in that those Aborigines now in charge of Aboriginal affairs have as their first language of communication, Standard English. They have no desire and can see no reason to challenge the hegemony of this language. If they do write, they write in Standard English.

This is seen in the short fiction pieces published in the periodical *Identity*, under the editorship of Jack Davis. The majority of these are in Standard English, though a few have a strong degree of Aboriginality in their content. Reg Saunders was an author who contributed several short stories to *Identity*. One of these in Volume 2, number 10, 1976 is called 'Parabar The Shark, A story about the Tasmanian Aboriginals'. This is interesting in that it uses the form of the European folktale to tell an Aboriginal story which blends fancy and fact to create a sense of Aboriginal reality.

The narrative is about a girl called Rowra who goes to live with the sea people. The time is during the Invasion and the place Tasmania, Cape Portland. Life is idyllic — then the white sealers arrive and pursue a girlfriend of Rowra's. She escapes; but they follow her, massacre the men and kidnap the women. They are taken away to other strange islands, but are comforted by seeing the shark, Parabar, swimming by. In the story Parabar is a symbol which links the Tasmanian Aborigines, especially the women, to nature and to the sea. He does not hurt the women, but when a sealer falls into the water, he is instantly attacked.

The story is interesting in that it does not operate on the level of a modern European story with its use of rounded characters and psychologism, but on the level of a myth, or tale, hinging on an implied moral with the central preoccupation being Aboriginal-White relations. The characters are flat, of cardboard thinness and are there only to serve the tale, which revolves around Parabar, the shark. The shark in Australia is a fish of fear to Europeans; but in this story shark-as-menace is reversed to shark-as-protector. Parabar serves as a symbol to highlight the alliance Aboriginal people have with the forces of nature. Thus the story ends with the two women looking at Parabar's dorsal fin plying in and out of the water. They find this sight comforting. Saunders by this reversal has attempted to reconstruct in content an Aboriginal world, though his discourse is Standard English.

Such stories based on the structure of the European folktale work well and allow for a reading on different levels, unlike the 'realist' short story which relies on mimesis. It is so constructed that we may feel for a character, or a situation vicariously. In *Identity* most of the short stories are of this type. 'Stolen Car', by R. Chee (1977, 3 (3), pp. 29–33) begins:

> He was eighteen years old, thin and dark as an ancient snag, hidden in a river. Golden laughter of the sun shone from his yellow eyes and melted into his blond curly hair.

We might contrast this with the oral style of a narrative put down on cassette by the Western Australian activist Robert Bropho and later transcribed under the title, 'The Great Journey of the Aboriginal Teenagers' in *Limit of Maps* (1985, pp. 19–25):

> The days of old, back there in the yesterdays, in the past . . .
> for us, Aboriginal teenagers then, in the fifties, in the late
> forties, up into the early sixties . . . back there in the past.

In the former of these two beginnings we have what might be described as a typical beginning of a realist fiction piece. There is an inclination towards simile and metaphor which as I have pointed out before is rare in Aboriginal styles of discourse. In the latter we have a beginning signifying Aboriginal discourse in that it is purporting to tell it how it is, though the personal has been deleted even on a group level. This is so that Robert Bropho can extend a group of Aboriginal teenagers into being representatives of that whole generation. He thus extends the realist mode beyond realism and into the realms of symbolism. This use of symbolism may be contrasted with the approach of Chee with his reliance on metaphor and simile. The use of symbolism is an aspect of Aboriginal discourse, and this aspect is the one most likely to be lost in the editing process.

Robert Bropho's and Chee's narratives both stress certain aspects of the Aboriginal condition in Western Australia, but there is a bravado in Bropho's work missing from the other writer's work. Chee's story is tragic (is this another Europeanisation?), Bropho's story is not. It is symbolic even in the central action of journey reaching beyond fact into mythology. Bropho has used journey in an earlier work, *Fringedweller* (1980) to symbolise a spiritual quest — spiritual in the sense that the material result did not matter. He uses journey in this short sketch exactly in the same way.

The teenagers of his story by undertaking the journey together go through a form of initiation. By undertaking the 'great' journey, a bond is established between members of a male generation exactly as in earlier times happened during the initiation process. It is more than coincidental that the band of teenagers do a tour of Western Australia. This, as in the traditional initiation journey, enables them to locate themselves in their land. They form a psychic map of their country, but in these days this is not enough. The old ways are broken and essentially there is no strengthening of community ties through the process. The boys do not return in triumph to their camp, but pass on to Fremantle prison. And Bropho eschewing the white tragic for the Aboriginal matter-of-factness ends his account with:

> And that's where the journey of the teenage Aboriginals —
> that's us — in the late 40s through the 50s and early 60s ended
> up . . . and that's what us the teenagers in them days went
> through.

'Stolen Car' is different. Incident is piled on incident, all of which are structured towards the tragic ending. There is none of the sense of initiation in the central act, the stealing of a car, no group solidarity, only the triumph and despair of the individual as found in most modern European narratives:

Slender hands grip the wheel and he pushes the beautiful blue being to its limit . . . For the first time in a long while Johnny Moydan isn't being pushed around. He is in control, he is free, he is supreme—he is someone.

But the car gets out of control and he crashes. Chee ends his story with:

Pathetic Johnny. The shadowy, formless people watch from the footpath. Watched you and the banshee-wailing police car rush past, leaving just a wind in your wake.
And who remembers a wind?

R. Chee is or was the pseudonym of Archie Weller, the author of *The Day of the Dog* (1981), and his work has been criticised for lacking a certain degree of Aboriginality, of lacking a certain degree of acceptance of things as they are rather than as they should be. In *Going Home* (1986), his collection of short stories, there is again an emphasis on gritty realism which is gloomy. The Aboriginal characters approximate more to rootless lumpenproletariat than to fringe dwellers. Naturally, this may be the situation of modern day Aboriginal (especially Nyoongah) youth in Western Australia, but most writers of Aboriginality emphasise the positive rather than the negative. They seek to get beyond characters who are rootless without a feeling of future. These characters are losers with no chance of change, and though the dialogue is straight from the fringe camps, there is little that any community would wish to identify with, or accept. Kevin Gilbert might agree with these stories, as they do depict an Aboriginal lifestyle which agrees with his theory of 'the rape of the soul', though he would criticise the lack of a promise of a better future.

In *Living Black*, Kevin Gilbert writes in the introduction that the original aim of the book was to show the conditions of the Aboriginal people through their own testimony. He found this impossible to accomplish as Aborigines indulged in 'an automatic self-censorship' being deeply ashamed of 'what they know is the truth about their people today'. He then outlines a number of what he calls 'myths' which Aborigines propagate about themselves. These he lists as: a strong feeling of community, a lack of materialism, an ability to share, and deeply caring for their children. He then sums up what he believes to be the true position:

> Aborigines try to believe these fallacies about themselves because they won't face the truth. But you only have to go to any Aboriginal mission or reserve to see the truth: the lack of community spirit, the neglect and abuse of tiny children, and all the rest of it.

Archie Weller in his stories does show this state of affairs. A lumpenproletarianism of Aboriginal communities which creates a tension and duplicity in life which is nasty to say the least. Still, the writer of Aboriginality while knowing these things prefers to write about, or postulate a hope in the future. He or she sees these things as only temporary aberrations, and not as aspects of Aboriginal culture. They will automatically disappear if there is a return to pristine Aboriginal values, or in Kevin Gilbert's case in the creation of a new Aboriginal society.

Writers of Aboriginality are ideological writers. They are not content to be only reporters of the Aboriginal condition in contemporary Australia. They believe in a future of hope and this often, as in the case of Robert Bropho, leads to political action. Archie Weller, on the other hand, is situated in the mainstream of Australian writing, which is still strongly realist. Such writers are content to describe the present situations as they occur, and although there may be individual development, the community is not treated as a whole and capable of development out of the morass in which it finds itself. His writings are closely related to such white writers as Thomas Keneally and his *The Chant of Jimmy Blacksmith* (1972), in which Aboriginal society is pictured as completely decayed. For the writer of Aboriginality this is not so. Many of the short stories in the periodical *Identity* although they may depict nasty situations, always end on a positive note. We Aboriginal people are a great race of survivors and this comes across in our literature.

9

Acting Fringe

One day I realised I was earning my living off misery row.

Bobby Merrit

A CONTINUING DREAM OF THE FAMOUS KOORI ACTOR, BRIAN Syron was the establishment of a national Aboriginal theatre. In 1987 together with the actress Justine Saunders, he organised the first black theatre conference and workshop in Canberra. Many actors, actresses and writers attended this convention and the result was the formation of the Aboriginal National Theatre Trust (ANTT) based in Sydney. This has been extremely active and has put on a number of shows including *Not the 1988 Party*, a good natured protest on the Australia Day celebrations for 1988.

Forerunners to ANTT were the Black Theatre of Redfern which produced Gerry Bostock's *Here Comes The Nigger* which unfortunately has never been published in its entirety, and the Nindethana Theatre in Fitzroy, Victoria which performed Kevin Gilbert's *The Cherry Pickers* with an all Aboriginal cast. In Perth, the Aboriginal playwright and poet, Jack Davis has his own company, Marli Biyol, as has Richard Walley (Middah Theatre Group), whose play *Coodah* was the only play workshopped at the Black Theatre conference to achieve full theatre production. Aboriginal theatre therefore appears very healthy at least in Sydney and Perth. It is difficult to write about theatrical productions so I shall confine myself to published Aboriginal plays.

A major reason for this is that I may ascribe the written text to the playwright, though I remain conscious that often the final text is the result of a group effort owing to the practice of workshopping plays. Another reason is that Aboriginal plays have often been directed by an Anglo-Celt; Jack Davis, for example, has established a warm relationship with Andrew Ross. Black or Aboriginal theatre at present seems to have entered a post-separatist period. Aborigines and Europeans happily cooperate to write and produce plays, and the situation may be summed up in the final words of Jack Davis' life story:

> It is a real pity that so much of the history of European-Aboriginal relations can be characterised by conflict and denigration. The initial Aboriginal response to settlement was one of cooperation. It would have been a much richer country in terms of culture—and conscience—if that cooperation had been reciprocal.

'Literature' essentially is language structured into some kind of genre and given permanency by being printed into a book or recorded on to tape. It is with this in mind that I will keep my examination to those plays which have been published with emphasis on two volumes of drama, *Kullark and The Dreamers*, by Jack Davis, and *The Cake Man*, by Robert J. Merritt. I turn my attention towards how these texts have been published.

The covers of these two volumes are similar in that the titles are displayed at the top in upper case letters. In Davis' volume this is followed by: 'Introduced by H. C. Coombs with an account of the Nyoongah people of South-Western Australia by Ronald M. Berndt'. Merritt's volume is treated in much the same way: 'Introduced by Mervyn Rutherford, with a preface on the stage history by the Author and historical notes on the Wiradjuri tribe of NSW'. After this comes the names of the playwrights.

This packaging of Aboriginal plays may be contrasted with the packaging of an American play I have on hand. The cover is very simple and states without fuss: *The Apple*, a play by Jack Gelber (New York, Grove Press, 1960). It is left to remark that this cover is decorated with five irregular large black dots in a triangular shape with a red

dot in the centre of the base line. This may be contrasted
with the Aboriginal play volumes. The Davis edition has
the face of an Aboriginal adolescent painted with white
streaks, and the Merritt edition has the smiling open face of
an Aboriginal boy. The paint streaks lead me to believe that
there will be traditional elements in the former and perhaps
none in the latter. This is borne out when I read the texts.

Although *The Apple* when published was an experimental play, it has no introduction. I expect that it was felt
that the text of the play would prove introduction enough,
but as for the Aboriginal plays, they are framed by introductions, and it is legitimate for us to ask why this has been
done. Is there a lack in the texts, or if there isn't, what
precisely is the function of these introductions.

H. C. Coombs in his introduction: 'An Invitation to
Debate', invites the reader to read the texts in certain ways,
though his words are not about the dramas. It is as if he has
not read, or seen the plays. He invites us to join in an
Aboriginal-settler dialogue. The Aborigines have reached
the stage of being able to open such a dialogue, but this has
not been met by Europeans. He then goes on to say that an
Aboriginal intelligentsia has arisen. He describes them
thus:

> Men and women who have seized upon what our society can
> offer them in education and access to the ideas of our
> civilisation . . . It is remarkable the degree to which these men
> and women have chosen to seek their careers and the measure
> of their achievement in the service of their own people and in
> the institutions they are creating.

He makes no mention of those Aborigines who have
rejected these ideas and seek to find their sources of inspiration in Aboriginal culture. He seeks instead to pull
Aboriginal artists and writers into *his* 'intelligentsia', and
writes of the emergence of new Aboriginal art forms:

> Naturally, these forms take over much of the structure of those
> of our own society. But in purpose, in content and in style,
> Aboriginal artists make them distinctively their own.

He does not write about how it may be possible that Aboriginal artists though now on the fringe of white 'civilisation' may make a contribution in structure by returning to their cultural roots. This is not important to him, for H. C. Coombs sees Aboriginal artistic productions as being 'consciously and unconsciously directed at us'. He sees them as an invitation towards a debate, 'a search from which some sense of shared identity may one day come'. This is partially true. But, although the theatrical audience is usually white and middle class, dramatists such as Jack Davis also write for their own people. They provide an opportunity for fringe dwellers to see themselves for the first time holding centre stage and talking back to the white man. This is an important aspect of such plays. Aborigines are enabled to see themselves and their history portrayed in positive terms, though in an environment and a structure with which they must come to terms.

The anthropologist Ronald Berndt's introductory piece is titled 'The Aboriginal History'. This is of importance in that while eschewing any discussion of Aboriginal dramatic structure, he writes about the language, and how Jack Davis uses in his play Aboriginal discourse in the shape of neo-Nyoongah as spoken in the South-West of Australia. He goes on to separate this neo-Nyoongah, which he calls Aboriginal-English, from Standard Australian English. He also, perhaps because he is an anthropologist, attempts to see the play from an Aboriginal perspective, that is from a viewpoint of Aboriginality, thus:

> Pride in being Aboriginal is indelibly inscribed in his writing, indicating firm roots which go deeply within the total Australian scene, far beyond the recent past, into its very beginnings.

From both these texts I, as a reader, am invited to accept the two plays in the volume as products of an Aboriginal writer who is committed to his people and who writes with a purpose. He is a writer of Aboriginality using Aboriginal speech forms, though he has as yet not structured his plays on Aboriginal forms. This lack does make for European type plays which European audiences may follow without any difficulty, but there there is little discussion of the plays as theatre.

Robert Merritt by writing a foreword to the second edition of his drama captures the textual space usually reserved for a white person. He invites the reader to see his play in certain ways. This begins idealistically in that he states that theatre was part of the natural way of Aboriginal culture before it was shattered, but he does not define what this theatre was, or is, and ignores any discussions about the form or structure of *The Cake Man*. It is noteworthy that in the first edition there was an afterword from the white director of the first production who was aware of the difficulties involved in producing a play which did not fit into the accepted genres of European drama. He discussed the first scenes, symbolic as much Aboriginal narrative is, which flowed into the straightforward, naturalistic, or realist body of the drama. Knowing little about Aborigines, the director saw this not as a continuing presence of Aboriginal modes of discourse on a structural level, but as a weakness in the drama, which actors and audiences accustomed to European theatre found difficult to accept. It is of interest that in the second edition this afterword was dropped, and the first scenes remain as an integral part of the play.

After the foreword by the playwright, there is a second introductory text which is a reminiscence of a European who knew the mission, 'Erambie', in which Robert Merritt grew up. By recounting his memories, this person in effect asks the reader to see the play in a certain way, as a realistic piece of writing or theatre:

> Robert Merritt's play *The Cake Man* depicts with accuracy in dramatic form a past way of life as we both remember it from when he was growing up in the 60s. It is still the present for too many people in Australia.

Thus the symbolic beginnings and the symbolic elements which continue throughout the play are ignored and I am asked to accept the play as an autobiographical piece.

The last introductory text reinforces this way of reading

the play. It describes the real setting of *The Cake Man* and then details the history of the people and the settlement. Strangely this piece ends with a long notation from Dr H. C. Coombs describing a traditional Aboriginal ceremony, the recitation of a song cycle. This in effect is contradictory in that it sets up a traditional dramatic scene which may be contrasted to the modern theatre of Robert Merritt.

From these framing texts, it is possible to read what type of plays I shall be confronting. They will be essentially realistic pieces of theatre in the European tradition. They have a message to impart, and they are for both Aboriginal and non-Aboriginal. This to a certain extent is what I do get, and taking my cue from the introductory pieces it is possible that this may be all that I shall get.

Robert Merritt in 'Impact', a program televised on the ABC, the National Government Television channel, on the 13th September 1986, established his view of the social importance of theatre. He described his newly founded centre, 'Eora Centre', where he sought to build up the self-esteem of Aboriginal young people in Redfern, a suburb of Sydney, where little traditional culture remains. He hoped that such centres would lead to a renaissance, or revival of Aboriginal culture. Part of the program was devoted to his centre, and there is a revealing sequence in which a group sit and watch a film of a traditional performance. For me this showed the gap between urban and country culture.

In the urban environment of Sydney, the roots of Aboriginality have withered and traditional culture has little relevance to young city Aborigines. Time, distance and place have given this culture an air of unreality. In its place the city Aborigines are trying to re-establish, or re-form a culture containing elements of the old and the new, though city experiences are more immediate than the old culture.

This is different in the case of Jack Davis. In Western Australia traditional culture continues to be strong in country places and migrates down to Perth with the seasonal movement of the people. There is contact and connection between old and new, between country and urban, and from the still performed Aboriginal ceremonies it is possible to reconstitute Aboriginal structures in a modern city environment, so that works may be produced Aboriginal in form as well as content.

Robert Merritt in seeking a renaissance of Aboriginal culture in an urban sprawl like Sydney, must first nurture his artists before achieving any sort of cultural revival incorporating important elements of traditional Aboriginal culture. He must first create again the artists which in traditional Aboriginal society made that culture creative and a source of strength. He sees 'The Eora Centre' as being the spiritual birthing womb for the creation of such artists. In an interview by Debbie Kruger, in the *Weekend Australian Magazine*, 18th and 19th October 1988, he said:

> Through the Eora Centre . . . I see the emergence of the artist—artists are going to keep our culture alive. I want to nurture those artists just like powerful societies do with their generals, because they're the people with a vision.

Robert Merritt's call for his students to become naked when acting recalls the approach to theatre by the so-called 'poor theatre' of modern Western drama. Jerzy Grotowski in an interview published in his *Towards a Poor Theatre* (1968) accents a certain 'holiness', a certain development of the individual in much the same way as Merritt does in the television program on his centre. This approach is very similar to the various group encounter sessions of personal development and even the acting out of problems as advocated by certain psychiatrists, though there is a difference in that the confrontation of the individual as actor with the audience—again as individuals—is de-emphasised in Merritt's approach with the group-as-audience assuming a supportive role which may reflect remnant traditional Aboriginal culture in that dramatic performances were essentially communal. They were group performances which were enacted not for any individual advancement, but for community health and well-being.

This accent on community rather than on individual is found in many rural and traditionally oriented communities where theatre is put at the service of the community as a source of spiritual and physical healing with the emphasis being on leading an alienated or sick individual back into the community. Usually, performances are held by the community for this purpose and, if not symbolic, are mimetic when certain areas of concern are identified. Thus the dramatic performances put on within the centre by the students reflect this tradition, though modern Aboriginal dramas put on in the theatre-as-building may not have this attitude.

Modern Aboriginal drama on first reading may be seen as realistic or naturalistic in the European sense, though certain aspects of Aboriginal reality keep intruding to bring the genre identification into doubt. Supernatural, or surrealistic elements have a place in Aboriginal reality and these are seen in Jack Davis' *The Dreamers* where they are an integral part of the plot. In *The Cake Man* these are part of the dialogue and, though never intruding into the action, are so much a part of the drama that they tend to subvert the realist aspects. In fact it is the Aboriginality of *The Cake Man* which lifts it above such sordid social plays as *The Man From Mukinupin*, by Dorothy Hewett (1979).

In Aboriginal Australia, theatre of the European type did not exist. Popular entertainment and didactic performances were provided by music, song and oral narratives. Apart from these were the non-secular performances—intricate ceremonies which passed on the traditional wisdom. Dramatic elements were important in the performances in which myths were re-enacted, or rather danced out; but these were truly social manifestations with close communion between actors and spectators, and often the whole community took part in them. They were staged in a special arena with little scenery, though amongst some communities large bark paintings were used as backdrops. Costume, particularly body painting and props (sacred symbols), were important, either to strengthen the connection with the mythical past, or to symbolise ancestral divinities. The role of the songman, who was the stage manager or producer, was of the utmost importance in that he supplied the textual discourse of the drama. Often he carefully arranged rehearsals before staging the theatrical event.

Story telling was another dramatic event with the narrator using such props as leaves. In the journal of anthropology, *Oceania* (1952, 22, 3), the anthropologist Catherine Berndt even rendered one of these stories into English within a dramatic framework, though with the admission that she left out elements which did not fit into her conception of what constituted theatre.

Traditional dramatic elements are found in *The Dreamers*. It is the dancer who shifts the play out of an essentially realistic mode and into Aboriginal reality. In *The Cake Man* these elements appear from the first in the stylised opening scene where stereotypical figures mime a primal scene much as in traditional secular performances. It is notable though that the important element of dance is missing. This has been replaced by dialogue: a dialogue which has been influenced by the art of the storyteller. This is evident in the early narration of a myth, and again in the epilogue.

The beginning and ending of the drama are precisely those parts of the play which have been criticised as weakening it. This criticism based as it is on expectation of genre, refers to when the naturalistic genre is broken by the intrusion of non-European conventions, of Aboriginal reality and old modes of dramatic performance which are paralleled in the dialogue where there is a constant intrusion of non-English words and mythic elements which again threaten any genre recognition. It is the Aboriginality of the discourse and dramatic structures which weaken it as a European theatrical piece, and conversely it may be said that the reliance on European theatrical conventions weaken it as an Aboriginal theatrical piece.

Aboriginal dramatists are schizophrenic in that they must seek to please both non-Aboriginal and Aboriginal audiences. It is impossible for them to avoid this if they seek to have their works performed in the conventional theatre with its white middle class audience. It is because of this that the Aboriginal plays under consideration make important concessions to European theatrical conventions and tastes, such as having the Aboriginal discourse modified to avoid undue repetitions which Western ears might find tiresome, but we must keep in mind that as most Aborigines rarely venture into the theatre, their ideas on what constitutes theatre will be different from those of an educated European.

Until recently, the only European dramas that Aboriginal people saw were conservative plays staged in mission halls or town halls, and their reading of plays would have been those read in primary schools. This may be seen as limiting, but then it can lead to an escape from genre entrapment in that genre is a learnt, rather than a natural classification. Thus what we might expect from playwrights with such backgrounds is a mixture of genre, a lack of conforming to the dictates of theatrical convention, and this is what we find in Aboriginal plays, though with an increased familiarity with European theatre, unless there is a strong infusion of Aboriginality, Aboriginal playwrights might be expected to produce more genre-typified plays.

This appears to be the case with Jack Davis whose *Kullark* and *The Dreamers* were quite complex in time and structure, but whose third play, *No Sugar*, has become restricted to a naturalist genre, though it has been staged in the round with the audience being forced to move around the theatre to follow the unfolding of the action, and to actively participate in it. This is a way of presentation much closer to traditional Aboriginal theatre in that Aboriginal audiences are never passive spectators, but then again the restricting of time and reality to a historical period of the 1930s is a lessening in the Aboriginal structure and a stricter adherence to genre.

There are a number of signifiers by which we may distinguish Aboriginal from conventional Australian theatre. These make for an originality of theme and content. One is the sense of community, or even the portrayal of family as community. Individuals rarely exist in isolation, but are units in a collective which is constantly emphasised and reinforced at the expense of the individual. This is such a common denominator, that it is seen even in student pieces. In 1983 four student dramatic pieces were presented in an anthology of student literature, published by the

Leederville Technical College, and the action of all four pieces is set in the Aboriginal community or within the family with little interaction outside it. They are in the naturalistic or realist genre. I will give a brief sketch of these pieces as they contain many of the characteristics of the published texts we are considering.

The Meeting Place by Debra Ogilvie is set in an open area where a group of Aborigines meet. The characters are all Aboriginal except for the intrusion of two white policemen, symbols of an outside force unwilling to intervene in what they see as purely Aboriginal problems unthreatening to the majority peace. The theme is feminist, in that women not only appear willing to attach themselves to worthless men, 'mongrels', but after doing so, refuse to extricate themselves from the unpalatable relationships. Women appear as victims, and the piece tentatively examines a community problem: women bashing

Boogy Man Yarn by Karen Loo is again in an Aboriginal setting, and the student reaches into Aboriginal culture to establish as the main character a storyteller who narrates to a group of children a ghost story and ends up frightening himself half to death.

The Children Who Were Mischievous by Sonya Khan is a family setting with the title explaining the plotline. In this piece a narrator is used as a dramatic device.

A Play by Donna Blurton is again a family setting, i.e. an extended family dramatic sketch in which the members settle down to drinking and later begin arguing.

These four pieces share what is recognisably a trait of all Aboriginal drama: sense of humour. We may give examples of this humour by referring back to *The Cake Man* and the character Sweet William. This example is taken from near the beginning of the play (p. 12):

He poses proudly now:
See'n I'm a Kuri. The Australian Aborigine, that's who I am and what I am . . . made in England.
(*Pause*)
Oh! Speakin' of social welfare cheques, y'see that in the paper the other day? (*Ponderously*) The minister said that there is no

real evidence to the fact . . . that *some* blackfeller' *is* spendin'
their social on likker. They's buyin' booze. (*With a sigh*) Oh,
just like them Red Injuns what ruined 'emselves the same way
. . . at the firewater all the time. (*Sighing, nodding*) I know
it's a fact. Hang on there. (*He nicks offstage and returns with
a half flagon of wine. He drinks from it and smiles.*) The
social cheque came yesterday, thank Christ.

This stance, this self-deprecating humour permeates the
dialogue of the four student pieces, and the overwhelming
presence of alcohol is part of the dramatic action of two of
them. *The Meeting Place* is similar to parts of *The Cake
Man*, with the welfare cheque replaced by the pension
cheque. *A Play* is also centred around drinking with the
humour centred on it. The underlying tension beneath the
humour is revealed, though the connection between tension
and alcohol is not made.

Another signifier of Aboriginal drama is the pessimistic
ending. There is little movement towards a brighter future.
Things will always go on in much the same way as they
have been going on. This is the same sort of fatalism which
may be found in modern dramatic works by such writers as
Samuel Beckett. *Waiting for Godot* could well be staged by
Aborigines as it portrays, in much the same way, the tension
found in Aboriginal dramas. Characters are literally roped
together in an uneasy alliance as they wait for outside
deliverance which is not forthcoming. *Godot* and *Cake
Man* use similar symbols of divine intervention. In the
former it never comes, whilst in the latter it turns out to be a
white man with a box of groceries.

The ending of *The Cake Man* is a fair example of how
Aboriginal plays conclude:

Two realities
(*pause*)
An' I've lost one. (*Pause*) But I want it back I . . .
need it back.
(*pause*)
Not yours . . . mine.

Here that aspect of waiting is paramount. There is no movement towards going and getting or retrieving that reality, no thought that to capture or recapture that reality involves a mythical heroic quest into the Aboriginal reality. There is an aspect of cultural paralysis about Aboriginal drama which needs to be resolved: that although the problem has been defined and the quest announced, there is no movement into Aboriginality. There is the absence of a hero able to descend into the mythic earth of Aboriginality, regain the tjuringas (sacred symbols) of his community and bring these cultural treasures back into the modern Aboriginal theatre.

It is noteworthy that *Kullark* ends on the same note of pessimism:

Alec: Well, here's to us.
Jamie: An' thousands like us.

A ray of hope faintly beams when an actor enters to sing a gloomy song, the final stanza of which rings down the curtain:

> With murder, with rape, you marred her skin,
> But you cannot whiten her mind.
> They will remain my children forever,
> The black and the beautiful kind,
> The black and the beautiful kind.

But this hope is nothing but survival, there is nothing of renewal, of rebirth in it. In Jack Davis' latest play *Barungin*, published in 1989, even this theme of endurance is threatened. The drama seeking to deal with and understand the many deaths of Aborigines in the gaols of Australia, ends with one of the characters reading out a long list of those who have died. It is a poignant ending which reminds me that although Aborigines may be seen as a great race of survivors, individually we may also be seen as a great race of victims.

10

The Buggared Fringe

I N HIS ARTICLE 'BLACK POLICIES' (*ABORIGINAL WRITING Today*, 1985) Kevin Gilbert stresses the job of the Aboriginal writer in these words:

> An onus is on Aboriginal writers to represent the evidence of our true situation. In attempting to present the evidence we are furiously attacked by white Australians and white converts, whatever their colour, as, 'Going back two hundred years . . . the past is finished . . .!' Yet, cut off a man's leg, kill his mother, rape his land, psychogically attack and keep him in a powerless position each day—does it not live on in the mind of the victim? Does it not continue to scar and affect his thinking? Deny it, but it still exists.

Kevin Gilbert is the strongest, toughest and most political of all Aboriginal writers and has struggled all his life for justice and rights for himself and his people. White critics in evaluating his works, often choose to ignore the political message to concentrate on the form, or structure. Supposedly cognisant with Aboriginal history, they may write on Gilbert as not being familiar with his language, that is the language of his tribe, the oral traditions of his tribe, and with the failure to list the origins of Aboriginal words he does use. What they fail to point out is that Kevin's people on both sides of the colour line have suffered oppression, and that the Wiradjuri people of New South Wales suffered under a constant pressure which resulted in their language being destroyed except for remnant words.

It is impossible to write about Aboriginal writing in English without an understanding of the history of Aboriginal people and of the policy of assimilation which cut the linkage to traditional culture and language. Thus Aboriginal writing in English is precisely Aboriginal writing in English because of that history, which is as bleak as the period spent by Gilbert in the prisons of the white man. In these times of text being supreme, and if not the text, the act of reading, the individual act of production by the author or writer is downplayed. You read the text for the text rather than reading the text for an understanding of the author and his message; but, in some unfashionable fringe areas of criticism, it is held that all writing is autobiographical, and that what the reader is confronted with is a continuing dialogue in the writer's mind. If the reader simply relies on the text, the whole act of communication between writer and reader is lost.

Literature as communication between writer and reader is important in my approach to Kevin Gilbert. Through his identification with the black cause his individuality, as it were, is submerged within the movement; but it must never be forgotten that he as an individual and as an Aborigine is the Aboriginal, and that his writings may be taken to be as much about himself as about his people. His history and his sufferings are as much their history and their suffering, as their history and their sufferings are his. It is a question of who is speaking, who is writing which defines the work of Kevin Gilbert. A definition by question which brings into focus the role of the writer, and especially the role of the Aboriginal writer trapped in word play and structures of genre and composition which he has had no part in forming, and which he often sees as being distant from him.

For this reason many Aboriginal writers are free from genre identification and select what the job demands, or what tool they feel is useful for the task. Thus Kevin Gilbert is an essayist, a polemicist, a poet and a playwright, and none of these. He is even Gilbert the murderer if occasion and slander demands, or Gilbert the politician, or jailbird, or take your pick. What I am most interested in, as I am approaching Kevin Gilbert through language and the texts ascribed to him, is Kevin Gilbert as writer, or wordsmith, or even Kevin Gilbert as constructed in his books. If the reader has not met the flesh and blood man, all that he or she may know about him, must be taken from the act of reading. Kevin Gilbert thus becomes a text for us to decipher as much as any other text.

First of all we may approach his volume of poetry, *People Are Legends* (1978). The cover is dark and sombre, easily blending into the fringe shadows of a second-hand bookshop. The shadows which go to make up the illustration of a child may be easily lost. One eye peers out at us while the child pensively sucks its thumb. In bright yellow in upper case lettering are the words PEOPLE and LEGENDS. Between the two words and of the same size and type font is a white ARE, and below the LEGENDS in white, though of a smaller size, are the letters spelling out the name: KEVIN GILBERT. The yellow of people and legends stands out and if you are an Aborigine, the bright colour reminds you of the yellow sun in our flag, the yellow sun representing the hope of a bright future. This symbolism is opposed to the meaning of 'legend' which my dictionary spells out as 'a traditional story, myth, such literature or tradition' and thus of the past. The white 'are' of the title is in the present tense. The verb is a doing word and the colour white reminds me of the Europeans always doing things, either to themselves, to the world, or to other peoples. The name, Kevin Gilbert, also in white is a part of the doing, that whiteness: it is his book of verse.

I learn little of Kevin Gilbert from the cover; though it is disturbing, and that single eye, that child's eye appears to have a certain quality of distrust about it. On turning the page, I see the cover blurb and begin to read. I find out that Kevin Gilbert is a poet and a journalist; *poet* coupled with *journalist* to emphasise the commitment of the writer. This 'commitment' is stressed, for I learn that his life's work bears witness to the anguish, the shame, and the glory of *his* stubbornly surviving people. The blurb goes on in this vein, and for once the humanity of the fringe is emphasised; but strangely the oppressor is not named.

There are no signifiers used to allow me to name this oppressor. Instead, Kevin Gilbert is constructed as a text individualised, but also identified with people. The long first paragraph ends with a signifier, stressed with inverted commas that Kevin Gilbert's verse is authentic verse, without any recourse to 'culture'. 'Cultured' verse, at least in this reading, is not authentic verse, and 'culture' is modified further by *politeness* and *hypocrisy* which are opposed to *living, love and humour*. This authenticity is emphasised with the phrase *without editing*.

I learn little of Kevin Gilbert in this long paragraph, but it is followed by a second paragraph in which biographical details are given. This gives me the necessary signifiers which define Aboriginal writers. He is born, as are most if not all Aborigines, in Australia and is firmly set in historical existence by being born in 1933. He has the usual primary school education and the work I would expect: a station hand. Then I am informed that he is a murderer and has spent fourteen and a half years *behind bars* and five years and seven months of this time in the notorious Grafton *goal*. This misprint is important and even leads on to the next sentence in which he is redeemed by *access to books*, and so his career as 'writer', modified by *Aboriginal*, begins.

His work is given the seal of approval by the intrusion of a quotation from a person named Stewart Harris, who writing about his previous book, *Because a Whiteman'll Never Do It*, informs me that Kevin Gilbert is a politician, modified by the adjective *Aboriginal*. The cover blurb then ends with a direct quotation from Kevin Gilbert in which we are informed that he is working as a nursery man and art gallery proprietor to gain finance to advertise the Aboriginal cause and '*one day, hopefully, to gain the freedom to further my playwriting and art*'. Thus Kevin Gilbert is constructed for me and with this information I can pass on to the poems.

When I turn to the title page, I find that I will not be reading ordinary poems, but 'Aboriginal poems'. What is it which makes them Aboriginal? They are obviously written by an Aborigine, for I have read this and they are about Aborigines, and in the language, returning briefly to the cover blurb, of 'living Aborigines'. This statement is legitimised by the publisher, the University of Queensland Press. What this language is I learn from the contents page. The first poem has the title, 'Baccadul', an Aboriginalised English word (tobacco) but all the other poem titles are in English with the only Aboriginal language words being proper nouns. The overall impression I receive from my reading is that the language spoken by living Aborigines is English, or dialects of English.

There are sixty-nine poems, a symbolic number and an example of *black* humour, an example of the human side of the question, as the cover blurb has informed me. The poems cover the whole range of historical Aboriginal experience, and the warping of an entire people is laid at the feet of the white man, the oppressor. At last he is identified for me! As I read the poems, I find the language is terse and bald and bereft of those comforting illusions of simile so beloved by the 'cultured' poet.

The first poem, 'Baccadul', refers to the slave wages paid for an Aboriginal worker. Other titles refer to the dismal handling of the Aborigine at the hands of the white oppressor: 'Soft Sam' has the theme of hunger; 'Fair Swap', exchange value based on mistrust; 'Maureen', white oppression and female suppression; 'Duffed', the same; 'Lover's Lament', the same. These poems extend out into a litany of man's inhumanity to man, and man's inhumanity to women. There is little hope, but what hope is there for the buggared fringe?

From poem twenty-four, 'Birth Control for Blacks', facets of modern Aboriginal life and the conflicts within the community become the subjects of the verses. Again there is the absence of hope, and from my reading of Kevin Gilbert-the-text I am entitled to ask has the experience of prison, of the 'goal' of Grafton resulted in a flawed text producing flawed poems, or has the abysmal reality of Aboriginal life in Australia led to the production of this poetry, or again is it a mixture of both? Could the buggared fringe produce verses less bitter than these in which the language flattens, tautens and tenses until the approach is close to the structure of nursery rhymes. We are in the presence of: *Mirror, mirror on the wall, who is the fairest of them all? Not you, you're Black!*

These questions may be extended to all poems written from the fringe, and I deepen my reading of them to include the writer behind the poems. I have hinted at this in my observations on the work of Jack Davis. Being born in a white world is no joke for a black man or woman. A primary school education in which we suffer and react to racist taunts, the psychical and physical blows of assimilation, the coming to terms with one's Blackness, the discovery of one's Aboriginality and the rebellion against a life of oppression — all these result in the formation of a writer with a message to get across. Message determines form, and this results in a straightforward verse structure. This is what is needed, not the repetitions and symbolism of traditional Aboriginal verse.

These are black words on a white page: messages crossing over to Black and White. Simplicity is not the result of the lack of a formal education, as stated by white critics with the implication being that if only they had been educated in the complexities of European verse, if only they had not been Aboriginal, they would produce poetry closer to a European standard and thus able to be judged by that standard. To these critics 'protest', this telling 'how it is', is not poetry. Thus the inventors of something called a 'prose poem' deny the legitimacy of rhythms and rhymes simple and direct as nursery rhymes; simple and direct as you find in traditional song types across the world. Also these verses are criticised for not having the 'rich rhythms of traditional Aboriginal society'; but where message is more important than form, these rhythms would get in the way. The reader could eulogise over the structure without determining the message. My recent volume of poetry, *Dalwurra* (1988) based on traditional song texts has been criticised by Aborigines precisely because of this.

Kevin Gilbert is not concerned with inventing new patterns. Intent on the message, he utilises certain traditional rhythmic patterns of Europe. These suit his message as many readers are familiar with them. Thus, the aesthetics of the poetry does not get in the way of the message. Not only this, but the verse structures he uses continue to be used outside the circle of the poets in good standing. They belong to a folk tradition which although localised in Britain still serve as legitimate forms for working class poets. They are part of a continuing tradition and are used by people believing that the words are more important than the pattern in which the words are placed. Kevin Gilbert simply makes use of this tradition as has Oodgeroo Noonuccal.

Kevin Gilbert's books are never prefaced by the words of a seemingly sympathetic White. He mistrusts such patronage; but it is impossible for him to escape the conventions of 'author'. An author or writer is constructed. He or she must be described, in effect must become language in order to exist for me as a reader.

I have already described how Kevin Gilbert was presented in *People Are Legends*, now I turn to *Because a Whiteman'll Never Do It*, which was published about four years before the poems, though the verse was probably written earlier. The cover of the book is plain, in red and gold letters on a black background—the colours of the Aboriginal flag—though Kevin's name is in white as on the cover of the verse volume and, as I have said before, this is because white is a symbolic colour of 'doing', and Kevin is a doer. His name too is different from his later books. He is Kevin J. Gilbert which perhaps has a nicer ring to it than a straight Kevin Gilbert, though it might cause some doubt in a reader's mind as to the identity of the two Gilberts. If I was to venture an extreme and see each text as different, I might identify this Kevin J. Gilbert as another author, perhaps a brother as his life is very similar to that of the poet. The author-text is a short publisher's note:

Descended from English/Irish stock on one side and from the tribes of the Kamilaroi and the Wiradjuri in New South Wales, on the other, Kevin J. Gilbert was orphaned at the age of seven—he quickly learnt what it meant to be black and poor in Australia. In 1957 he was sentenced to penal servitude for life for the killing of his European wife. He served fourteen and a half years in Her Majesty's prisons — institutions of which, he says, she is perhaps not as ashamed as she should be. Self-educated in jail, he became an accomplished artist in oils and linocut, a poet, a dramatist and writer. He has used these abilities to demonstrate to white Australians the injustice and inhumanity that they continue to tolerate toward his black race. Kevin Gilbert sees this book as 'an attempt to make a contribution towards the regeneration of the Aborigine . . . in a land that may, one day, at last become big enough to hold a people who have been dispossessed for nearly two hundred years'.

This note sets up the text of Kevin J. Gilbert. It gives him a reality to the reader. First of all I learn that he is a mixture of 'stock' and 'tribes'. Even today this invokes an opposition in that tribes are considered primitive, whereas stock is considered civilised. Europeans are not seen as descending from tribes. They have surpassed this primitive stage of human evolution; but other peoples, such as the Aborigines are descended from primitive tribes. 'Stock' is a signifier of civilised and conjures up the placid nature of Europe populated by sleek animals bred for a purpose and thus of better quality than the wild. Binary oppositions continue from this first sentence.

As I progress in my reading the character is built up for me. I learn that he is poor, an orphan, a Black, a murderer, but in opposition to these negativities, these blacknesses, are placed the positive attributes stemming from the civilised stock, for after all these marks of civilisation are European: *accomplished artist, poet, dramatist, writer.* The blackness of his tribal side is downplayed, an accident to be dismissed, and the anger and subject matter of the book belongs to the white stock attribute: 'He has used these abilities to demonstrate to white Australians the injustice and inhumanity that they continue to tolerate toward his black race'. This sentence in itself is interesting in that injustice and inhumanity are tolerated by white Australians, but no mention is made of the inflicting of these inhumanities by white Australians. By adroit use of language, the settlers are rendered guiltless except for a psychological attitude which may be eradicated by education. Here is the danger faced by an Aborigine when playing the publisher's game. By entering the white halls or offices of the publisher, he is leaving himself open to covert manipulation. Mudrooroo too has left himself open to manipulation.

A careful reading makes it possible to divide the publisher's note into binary oppositions:

WHITE	BLACK
US	THEM
English/Irish	Kamilaroi/Wiradjuri
Stock	Tribes
	orphan
	black
	poor
European wife	prison
artist/poet/dramatist	murderer
abilities	injustice
toleration	inhumanity

I find that this note compromises Kevin J. Gilbert and contructs him as a white text for public consumption; but to achieve publication always involves compromise and Kevin's words challenge such compromises. His text is a polemic directed at the injustices inflicted by the white invaders on the indigenous people of this country. In opposition to the publisher's note, it is dedicated to those Aboriginal patriots who have refused to sell out, and his main text is followed by an author's note acknowledging the compromises he had to make to have his book published. This in effect continues the opposition detailed above; but ironically so that there is a reversal in that, while acknowledging the powerlessness of Aborigines such as Kevin J. Gilbert to change things, a fierce independence is maintained, though owing to the fact that much has been left out, this in some ways is a sham. It exposes that to be 'white' published is a compromise and a lack of independence. Kevin cleverly makes this lack of independence the subject of his book. To be born Black in Australia is to be born powerless, is to be born into the negativities of blackness as defined by the Whites.

Kevin's book exposes the historicity of the Aborigines in Australia in which the oppressors hold all power and dominate history. Aboriginal accounts are only memories captured on a tape-recorder: footnotes below the glosses of official white history. It is significant that the voice of the Aborigine is heard in verse at the beginning of each chapter. This serves to emphasise the unhistoricity of the powerless. The powerless have no recourse to the prose of history. They are not writers, but victims unable to construct their own history. They have only their memories passed on as stories whispered in the night or songs singing out protests which may be slurred over in dialect. An anthropologist once declared that it was a good thing to let the Blacks sing, for it showed that they were content in their camps away from the houses of the settlers. But Kevin Gilbert has written this book, has captured prose for his own use. The job of the Aboriginal writer is to give his people a history.

The structure of *Because a Whiteman'll Never Do It*, with the use of poetry and prose, is reminiscent of an English eighteenth century political pamphlet. There is the device of directly addressing the reader as in this example:

> White man, you may well speak to the Aborigine of your 'democracy' and 'justice' and 'Christianity'. But your reality is a little at variance with your theory. The Aborigine snarls his disbelief of your words as he slinks away unmanned.

There is an immediacy about the book which has not dated. The problems of the sixties are the problems of the eighties and they lie as heavy as the broken promises of the politicians.

Kevin Gilbert's most successful book which has gone through six editions or reprints is *Living Black: Blacks Talk to Kevin Gilbert* in which the position of the author, or writer is ambiguous in that the cover both emphasises and denies his authorship. The cover is black and at the top large white upper case letters declare LIVING BLACK. Perhaps the use of the black backround has meant the automatic selection of white as the dominant colour, but underneath it in red, or rather orange, in much smaller upper case letters is: BLACKS TALK TO KEVIN GILBERT. Below it is a smiling portrait of Kevin Gilbert, though as the sub-title refers to his passive role, it may be asked why a group shot of Blacks has not been shown, as they are signified to be the true authors, or writers of the work.

The conventions of authorship create confusion. A book in the majority culture needs a single author and on opening the volume, I am presented with the author, Kevin Gilbert-as-text. This follows what by now I am accustomed to, at least until near the end, where after it is declared that Kevin Gilbert is the first Aboriginal playwright, he is described as a poet, a great talker, an oils artist, and the author of *Because a Whiteman'll Never Do It*, the first major political work by an Aboriginal. Thus Kevin Gilbert is fleshed out for me. However, I note that he is described as being descended from Aboriginal, Irish, English stock, thus eliminating the racist opposition noted before.

The book is prose and purports to be transcripts of interviews of a large number of Aboriginal people by Kevin Gilbert between October 1974 and August 1976. When we examine the interviews the ambiguity of the writer, or author, or interviewer is manifest in that the style of the speakers is not the 'ums' and 'arrhs', the false starts and abrupt transitions of a truly oral style. They have been doctored to give the impression of being oral discourse. This explains the ambiguity of the author as signified on the book cover. It does not detract from the veracity of the interviewees, only the author, though 'author-as-interviewer' does have a prominent place in the production, part of which is to provide an introduction giving his reasons for 'writing' the book:

> I have also written this book in order to bring white Australia to some greater compassion through understanding and to enlighten it to its responsibilities in the areas of land and compensation for Aborigines.

It may be argued that this is the purpose of all of Kevin's works and increasingly what has been published are political essays rather than literature. He is a deeply committed writer and a writer of Aboriginality who uses words as tools to get his points across to both Blacks and Whites. The development of an authenticity of author and style is beneath his interest. Language is for communication and not for aesthetics. Being an author is not an end in itself, but an adjunct to social action.

I attended a Commonwealth Writers' Conference in Singapore, during which among the Black writers present, there was heated discussion on the role of the writer. One suggestion was that he should be a politician. Kevin Gilbert might agree with this, for the rhetoric of his style reflects that of the politician. The ambiguities of Kevin Gilbert as a writer are really the ambiguities of a politician. His concern is with the Aboriginal situation and the troubles of his constituents. This explains his use of the interview and his role of editor in a recent anthology of Black Australian poetry. He uses any personal creative expression only to elucidate a program suitable to eradicate a social evil.

It is worthy of note that in 1988 he was one of the few Black Australians to present a consistent program of Aboriginal advancement. He urged Aborigines to adopt a united policy towards the White majority and demand a treaty. It is a shame that the self-professed black leaders sabotaged this in favour of what can only be described as integration into white Australia. Thus one of the most astute voices of Aboriginal aspirations was stifled just when it was needed.

11

Disguising the Fringe

S TEPHEN MUECKE IN HIS INTRODUCTION TO THE TRAN-
scripts of Paddy Roe's stories, *Gularabulu* (1983, p. v)
comments:

> The translation from speech to writing, especially writing
> considered suitable for public consumption, involves editing
> which is massive in its proportions and implications.

This is true. From the beginnings of contact between the
two peoples, when Aboriginal oral literature has been
collected and then published little or no regard has been
paid to how it was told, that is to the discourse of the story.
Content was considered more important. Sometimes the
very ones at fault have been academics, linguists who
should have known better. Other Whites were exploiters
after a quick quid. They obtained a version of a story, then
rewrote it for publication as a children's story.

Often Aboriginal storytellers have been flattered by someone wishing to record their stories; others have wished to
share their cultural knowledge, and so quite a large amount
of material has been recorded. Some of this appears heavily
edited in books, the rest is scattered in institutions and
among private persons. There is a problem: who owns the
copyright of this material?

Anglo-Celts copyright their written versions and thus the

Aboriginal storytellers lose out in royalties. Linguists and anthropologists publish translations and edited versions of collected material under their own names. The Aboriginal storyteller is reduced to an informant who may get a mention in a footnote. His or her name rarely appears on the title page as the author. Perhaps one of the best things that has happened in regard to Aboriginal storytellers has been the establishment of the Australian Institute of Aboriginal Studies which, by becoming one of the main funding bodies for research, has managed to keep some sort of control over researchers and others exploiting the Aboriginal communities. Aboriginal people have often criticised the role of the Institute. This well-founded criticism has been constructive in that the Institute has been forced to listen to the desires of Aboriginal communities and to direct research into areas of Aboriginal importance.

It is often forgotten or ignored, that most of the Aboriginal people of Australia exist on the fringes of the majority culture. In country areas, especially around the towns in the northern part of the continent what is readily apparent are the racist attitudes which keep them there. The main attitudes are contempt and exploitation. This may be changing, but when I was in the Kimberley in 1984 and in northern Queensland in 1989, I observed that Aboriginal people suffer as a calcified colonised society. This means that many Aboriginal communities have ceased being living vibrant entities and have become the changeless primitive societies they were once postulated to be. Culture and society to live have to keep on growing, but this is not the case in many of these communities. A major reason for this is that they have no power to change their situation. Change is allowed, but this change comes from the outside and it is slanted always towards assimilation.

Assimilation at the social level is reflected on the language level. Aboriginal speech patterns are not acceptable and must be replaced by those of Standard English. This urge to do away with, and actually replace Aboriginal discourse is seen in such books as the so-called lifestory of Jack Sullivan, *Banggaiyerri* (Shaw, 1983), in which Aboriginal discourse and by this I mean Aboriginal English must be translated, that is assimilated into the Standard English discourse of white Australia. This translation reflects an ideal or ideological position in which Aborigines are to be forced into the majority culture. It is assimilation on the discourse level, though in actuality it does not mean that the Aboriginal person has the option of being assimilated. The stereotype of the *blackfellow* is still all pervasive in Australia and no matter what sort of English he or she speaks, he or she for all that is still a *blackfellow* or a *gin*. Assimilation is really not an escape from the fringe, but only a way of showing how unwelcome is the average blackfellow in the majority society.

If it is impossible for many Aborigines to assimilate completely into the majority culture, I ask myself if it is possible to escape back into traditional society. From what I have seen, traditional society has either become transitional society, or been made over into an artefact. It has become fossilised and the young people have turned away from the fossilised remains. Is it any wonder then that the institutions of their society have become objects of shame, ridiculous monuments of a stoneage culture. This is too evident in books such as *My Country of the Pelican Dreaming* (Shaw, 1981) which on a deep reading discloses such fossilisation together with the acceptance of a colonised condition. All effectiveness and social dynamism are monopolised by the coloniser's institutions. If an Aborigine needs help, it is to them that he applies; if he does something wrong, it is by them that he is punished; and if his story is to be written it is to be written by the coloniser, on the coloniser's own terms.

Even the education system belongs to the coloniser and reflects the things of Europe more than the things of Australia — with perhaps a few tokens of Aboriginality thrown in as a goodwill gesture. Fringe dwellers lurk on the outskirts of this system, and if they enter, they are taken in and escorted to their place. Children soon learn that they are being educated into that place. A foreign culture is thrust upon them and they recite words in a foreign tongue. If they fail to master Standard English, they are relegated into the language world of Kriol or Aboriginal English.

Those who do achieve fluency in Standard English fall into linguistic dualism. In a fringe situation, this bilingualism is necessary. Standard English is a condition for all culture, for all communication and progress. This language attainment is made a necessity for the Aborigine. It is to be their future, and because of this most, if not all, Aboriginal languages are on the defensive, as are the varieties of Aboriginal English which must be apologised for, or reconstructed, or translated, or explained. Rarely are they accepted. They are constantly under threat, under discussion and study.

The separation between native language and cultural language is not peculiar to the colonised; but it cannot be compared to just any linguistic dualism. Possession of two languages is not merely a matter of having two tools, but means the participation in two psychical and cultural realms. Two worlds are symbolised; two discourses are in conflict, and it is the mother discourse of the colonised which is devalued. In the past this devaluation of Aboriginal languages has led to the creation of new Aboriginal discourse structures such as Kriol or Aboriginal English which replaced or existed alongside the original language. This was one attempt at solving the language conflict, but it was not enough. A victory is called for, and victory goes to those with the strongest weapons. A sign appeared in the sky in 1986 with the launching of the AUSSAT communications satellite. The whole of Australia was flooded with the majority discourse of Standard English.

This signifier reveals the subordinate position of Aboriginal languages and Kriol. They may be taught in a few schools, heard on a few radio programs, but possession of them is not enough in Australia. If an Aboriginal person wants a job, wants to secure some sort of position, Standard English must be mastered. Everyone knows this, and so it is the Aborigines themselves, especially the young, who are discarding their languages. They feel ashamed of them, declare that they know them not, hang their heads as they mumble that they talk like everybody else.

If this attitude is taken into account, there is little wonder that in the two books I have mentioned, the subjects Jack

Sullivan and Grant Ngabidj surrendered their Aboriginal discourse, their voices to Bruce Shaw, the white recorder. In reality there was little choice. It was either this, or writing their own books, and their position made it difficult for them to even think of doing this. If they had done so, their life stories would have achieved a value not only to others, but to themselves. They would have become aware of their fringe place in Australia. This never happened and so in the books produced by Bruce Shaw we find little reflection on the politics of the fringe. It is only when we read those books by writers who have control of their writings, that the subordinate condition of the fringe comes in for examination. Thus authors like Bob Bropho and Labumore (Elsie Roughsey) by keeping control, by writing their own books, are able to question the white dominance.

When an Aborigine suddenly is confronted by a white person with a tape-recorder, it is only natural to expect a self-censorship to come into play. The Aborigine conscious of his subordinate position, is extremely careful to tell the white person what she or he expects to hear. The Aborigine suddenly becomes tongue-tied, suddenly hesitates as the past two hundred years of oppression weigh on his shoulders. He remembers the time when to open one's mouth, to speak the truth, could and often did mean death. His culture is filled with accounts of men opening their mouths to receive in exchange for their words of defiance a bullet.

Until the advent of Bob Bropho, Elsie Roughsey and Lionel Fogarty, the only way, apart from sitting down with a recording white man and giving him your words, was to write in Standard English. Thus the Aboriginal writer had to waste a lot of his creative imagination and energy in first attempting to achieve a proficiency, in acquiring a style acceptable to the speakers of Standard English. Even now, non-Standard English needs words of apology in Standard English. Thus Bob Bropho's book contains a publisher's note apologising for his Aboriginal English; Elsie Roughsey's book contains an afterword explaining away her language; and Lionel Fogarty must go outside the established publishing world to have his books printed. But even this marks an advance, for before Aboriginal writers had to express themselves in Standard English, that is they had to assimilate themselves into the mainstream, otherwise there would be no publication. But even when doing so they found that they could not just be a writer, or an Australian writer. They must always be Aboriginal writers, and were judged as Aboriginal writers and not on merit. Thus by writing, they became exposed to the contradictions set up by the assimilation policy in Australia. They found that there was no assimilation, except for the wound in their souls.

The Aboriginal writer exists in ambiguity. White people assume that he or she is writing for the white world, the world of the invader. It is a curious fate—to write for a people not one's own, and stranger still to write for the conquerors of one's people. Wonder has been expressed at the rancour in Kevin Gilbert's books. They have 'gifted' him their language and here he is using it to attack them, and they turn to the gentler Oodgeroo Noonuccal who accepts a common humanity; but the wonder is that any Aboriginal writer can write without the feelings of a Kevin Gilbert. Can words of peace or thoughts of gratitude be expected from someone who has had their own language stolen from them? They feel this tragedy in each and every word they write, but there is no going back, no return.

The assimilated writer has succeeded after much effort in making Standard English his own. Now he or she can only fully express himself or herself in it; while all the time supporting Aboriginal languages and clamouring for the complete use of Aboriginal discourse. This is a dilemma which Aboriginal writers seek to solve in various ways. Jack Davis, by turning to drama, has to a great degree escaped Standard English by using those elements of Nyoongah language which still remain. For other writers, especially those in urban situations, there may be no such escape. After a long apprenticeship in Standard English this, for the assimilated writer, is his or her mother tongue—and the use of non-Standard Englishes, Kriol and Aboriginal languages must be left to those newly arrived writers who can spontaneously express themselves in them.

For many years now, the majority culture has sought to image the fringe in dubious productions often termed 'autobiographies'. Altruistic motives often are given for producing these compromised volumes, though perhaps the main motive is economic. A fine example of this genre of 'life story' is *I, the Aboriginal* (1962), by Douglas Lockwood, who mined an Aborigine for source material. This is a journalistic production with the subject matter tightly controlled and rendered down for public consumption. The language is Standard English and I doubt that the '*I*' of the story had any say in its production.

Other Aborigines who became known to the majority, usually sportspersons, for example Lionel Rose, the boxer, and Evonne Goolagong, the tennis player, had their stories put down by journalists. These books were written to cash in on their popularity. Other biographies, such as those on the lives of famous Aborigines like Sir Douglas Nichols, were written by altruistic people for reasons such as to show the white majority that Aborigines were human beings capable of achievement, or to serve as models for Aboriginal youngsters.

Over the last few years, these life stories have again become popular. *My Place* by Sally Morgan (1987) has sold over 70 000 copies. This might be a sign that Aboriginal literature is moving from the fringe towards the centre. Perhaps; but if it is, it is moving into a place already created. This is 'the battler' genre. The plotline goes like this. Poor underprivileged person through the force of his or her own character makes it to the top through own efforts. Sally Morgan's book is a milepost in Aboriginal literature in that it marks a stage when it is considered O.K. to be Aboriginal as long as you are young, gifted and not very black. It is an individualised story and the concerns of the Aboriginal community are of secondary importance. I have already quoted in my introduction from *Wandering Girl* by Glenyse Ward which ends in an assimilationist affirmation.

If it was not for the neglected masterpiece, *An Aboriginal Mother Tells of the Old and the New* by Labumore (Elsie Roughsey, 1984), Black Australian women's literature might be seen as advocating assimilation; or else publishing companies are consciously publishing only those books which advance this ideology. Such has been the popularity of Morgan's and Ward's books that it has been suggested that Aboriginal literature is entering a post-activist period. This should be given some credence. In the important year of 1988, Aboriginal emphasis was on 'sharing and understanding' rather than on justice; many Aborigines participated in events celebrating the birth of white Australia and the death of black Australia, and the important Aboriginal writer, Oodgeroo Noonuccal staged a theatrical extravaganza at the Brisbane Expo, one of the highlights (though not officially) of the bicentennial celebrations.

In 1988, a number of Aboriginal books were funded, one of them *Don't Take Your Love To Town* by Ruby Langford. It was edited by a white woman, Susan Hampton. This is Koori literature and the life story at its best. It shows what can be done with the genre without being political. But then, the editor appears to have been deeply sympathetic to the style of Ruby. The work fits neatly into the 'battler' genre, as a quotation from the publisher's blurb will show:

> 'Born at Box Ridge Mission, Corkai in the 30s, Ruby
> Langford's story is one of courage in the face of poverty and
> tragedy.'

It should not be forgotten that the Aboriginal life story originated, not from biography or autobiography as might be supposed, but from social anthropology. In the middle of the 1960s, the taping of life stories (life histories) was popularised by the American anthropologist, Oscar Lewis, who turned his tapes into best sellers, possibly with the help of judicious and thorough editing. His *La Vida* (1965) is a delightful book, well worth reading.

The Australian anthropologist, Bruce Shaw followed the American lead to produce the two volumes to which I have already referred. These are essentially anthropological texts extending the methods of American social anthropology into Australia. His attitude to Aboriginal discourse is discussed in the introduction to *My Country of the Pelican*

Dreaming. His justification for rewriting the texts, which we must remember are anthropological texts is an excuse:

> Tampering with the original expressiveness worried me at first, until I realised that it was unrealistic to expect the general reader to wade through 200 pages written in the original style.

Shaw's 'general reader' can only be taken to be white. The nature of his 'general reader' must be queried as his books are published by the Institute of Aboriginal Studies which publishes books mainly for the academic reader, as a catalogue of its publications will reveal. There is a problem of ethics in that it is impossible to accept at face value the cover statement of the life story as being 'told to Bruce Shaw' when he has effectively transcribed, rewritten, and structured Grant Ngabidj's original discourse.

Stephen Muecke, another transcriber of Aboriginal narrative, refuses to tamper with original expression. He is deeply conscious of Aboriginal discourse and takes pains to render it down accurately; but his volumes, *Gularabulu* (1983) and *Reading the Country* (1984) barricade the discourses of Paddy Roe between slabs of Standard English. Paddy Roe is reduced to language, or discourse as heard through the ears of a European. Kriol or Aboriginal English becomes an interesting artefact which may be measured and deciphered using the methods of European criticism. In *Reading the Country* this has been pushed to such an extreme that Paddy Roe's discourse becomes imprisoned between slabs of academic prose resembling nothing more than the walls of a prison.

In these white productions there is an absence of critical and political comment on the part of the subject, and no analysis of Aboriginal-being-in-Australia—though a deep reading does disclose that existential being structured within the text itself. The fringe soul of the Aborigine peers out of his prison and reminds me of a shuffling Beckett character uttering parables into the recording apparatus of white dominance.

When an Aborigine becomes a writer and turns to writing his or her life story, I find a vastly different text in both style and subject matter. Labumore (Elsie Roughsey) wrote *An Aboriginal Mother Tells of the Old and the New* (1984), then watched it being changed by editors. But there was not the wholesale rewriting as done by Bruce Shaw, or the massive framing and intrusions of Stephen Muecke. Labumore retains control, as much as she is able, of her book, and there are reflections on the Aboriginal being in Australia, which are absent from the other productions:

> I wondered so much about all this. We have drifted so far away from that life, and have gladly marched forward into that life that really is hurting us, to care not to go any further. (p. 235)

When Aborigines begin writing and putting down their words, reflection and analysis becomes stronger, and although the immediacy of oral discourse is lessened, this in no way detracts from the Aboriginality of the text. I have only to compare Labumore's style with that of Shaw to see the difference in feeling and, in reading her book, there is no sense of ploughing through unfamiliar ground as Shaw would have us believe. It is the act of writing itself, of consciously or unconsciously being in control of your own material which makes for a stronger narrative. Writing is more important than a recording. It allows you to keep control of your material and recast it to your liking. This control is very important if a literature of Aboriginality is to grow.

I see the effect of this control in Bob Bropho's book, *The Fringedweller* (1980). This is the least tampered with of Aboriginal life stories and is mercifully free of long introductions, forewords, afterwords explaining, conceptualising and doing all sorts of things to Aboriginal discourse in exactly the same way as the white man has been doing physically to Aborigines since the first European ships sailed along our shores. All of the books which I have been discussing, except for *An Aboriginal Mother Tells of the Old and the New* (to a certain extent), are examples of white dominance and either Aboriginal acceptance of, or a seeking to come to grips with, this dominance. In this relationship of centre to fringe there is no equality, and what we are dealing with are essentially flawed texts.

Bropho's book is an exception to this dominance, and when there is an Aboriginal control of discourse, what I expect to find and usually do find is a mixture of genre, or an ignoring of genre. Aborigines when allowed to express themselves freely do not stick to European genre-types, and thus in *Fringedweller*, I am presented with mixed signals. It is both a polemic and an autobiography. Bob Bropho as fringe dweller expands outwards to symbolise all fringe dwellers. *Fringedweller* is not so much the story of Bob Bropho as of the people living on the fringe. Community is foremost, and the cover illustration is not the smiling face of the author, but a family pressed together into a collective whole.

12

Women of the Fringe

WE ARE BOSSES OURSELVES, WHITE-EDITED BY THE anthropologist Fay Gale and published by the Institute of Aboriginal Studies (Canberra, 1983) is an important work in that it frames Aboriginal women. I use the term 'frame' deliberately as I would like to begin with the illustrations in the book. These are important in that I am able to read from them the position of black women in both traditional, transitional and contemporary Australia.

Photographs and illustrations are texts which enable us to perceive how people are framed. For example the cover illustration of *We Are Bosses Ourselves* does not isolate a particular female individual, but is a group photograph. The women are not isolated in themselves, but share the space with one another and with their children. Men are absent and the photograph draws attention to the title: '*We Are Bosses . . .*' This type of group photograph occurs throughout the book and may be contrasted with those found in Bob Bropho's, *Fringedweller*. Community is emphasised at the expense of individuality. My reading of this illustration may be carried over to the examination of the life stories of women. In black women's stories, we fail to find the isolation we get in most male life stories. In fact in men's life stories, the male 'I' dominates the text. We find this even in Robert Bropho's text, though in the illustrations community is emphasised.

Apart from this, other illustrations in *We Are Bosses Ourselves* show the changes Aboriginal women have passed through. Those from mission days, for example, reveal how the women were framed in a typical patriarchal family. Usually the men as proud patriarchs stand towering over the women who are sitting. It is noticeable that a woman is paired with a single male and, a signifier of the female role, a child is clasped in her arms. A picture is worth a thousand words and this is certainly true of the way Aboriginal women were posed in these early photographs.

In traditional times, Aboriginal societies were rigidly divided into social sections. There was also a division between men and women. Women had their own rules of conduct and their own rites and ceremonies. Naturally, there was a reciprocity between the sexes, but women's business was women's business, and men's business was men's business.

When the Europeans arrived with their patriarchal society, the division changed. Women became subjugated to men and there arose one law for all, although women were treated differently from men. Their natural roles were stated to be those of mother and wife. The wife was considered to be under the rule of the man, the husband, and he could punish her with impunity.

As women have been treated differently in both black and white society, it is only a matter of accuracy to treat their writing as being different from that of men. In fact from my analysis of a number of women's stories we shall find that this is so.

We Are Bosses Ourselves is the proceedings of the First Australia-wide meeting of Aboriginal women held in 1980, and when I turn to the photographs of contemporary black women, I find a definite change from earlier illustrations. The female group breaks apart and women are framed doing things individually, though they are pictured in typical female roles of 'nurturing': teaching and nursing. Strangely, I find not one photograph of a black woman writer. This makes me suspect this book. If 'we are bosses ourselves', should we rely on a white woman to write us down. It may be, quoting from the cover blurb, that 'the book shows clearly that Aboriginal women are on the move and can and will speak for themselves and their communities'; but the omission puzzles me. A number of articles in the book have clearly been written. This is apparent from the style, and so the picture of a black woman writer should have been included. Returning to the cover blurb and the final sentence, 'our assumed knowledge and current prejudices will be shaken if we are prepared to listen', I might ask who is the 'we' referred to. The illustrations clearly place an emphasis on 'traditional' white female roles.

Black women have always been more than mothers, nurses or school teachers. At one time, Aboriginal women were protesting at the lack of men willing and able to help run our organisations. Women such as Dr Roberta Sykes, Oodgeroo Noonuccal, Gloria Brennan, Margaret Valadium, Margaret Briggs, Elizabeth Hoffman, Margaret Tucker and Faith Bandler have been at the forefront of the Aboriginal movement and a number of these are writers. In reading a text, we should always be aware of what is left unsaid as well as what is said, and so I ask, why this omission? A reason might be the anthropological nature of the text, or that an ideology of group collectivity or solidarity of women has been maintained at the expense of truth. The concept of women as a collective is an important aspect of contemporary feminine theory. This solidarity of women as an oppressed minority only recently removing their chains may be true, but woman-as-writer, especially black-woman-as-writer has been written out of this text. She remains hidden in her solitude.

This solitude is too real and is confronted by the black woman when she begins writing, even though her work may reflect specific women's concerns such as genealogy, the bearing and raising of children, or the management of an Aboriginal organisation.

When I read black women's life stories, I note immediately that there is a difference of voice and subject matter, though women's literature has suffered at the hands of well-meaning editors as much as that of men. It is only in the last few years that black literary texts have been allowed to speak for themselves: that is, the Aborigine is allowed to say what she or he wants to say and in the language she or he wishes it to be said. In this chapter I shall be concentrating on three black women's texts from Queensland, New South Wales and Western Australia. I shall begin chronologically, as this will show how books by Aboriginal women have been published over the last decade.

The first book *Through My Eyes* by Ella Simon has passed through two editions, 1978 and 1987. It is the autobiography of a detribalised Aboriginal woman in New South Wales. However, the book was white-edited. The cover features a close up of the author and reflects on the contents which are centred on the individual.

It seems to be a typical example of the 'battler' genre as Ella's problems as detailed in the book are overcome through strength of will. She wins through against all odds and projects herself as an example to other Aborigines. Both editions have been given legitimacy through forewords by well-known white authors. The first was by the well-known anthropologist, Professor A. P. Elkin, who ends his text with the words:

> I hope Aborigines will read this story of one of their number who blazed a trail through this maze of prejudice and fear. I urge non-Aboriginal citizens to read it and realise what Aborigines, especially those of mixed descent, have suffered in our midst.

Ella Simon did not like Elkin's foreword and in the second edition it was replaced by one by the noted white Australian poet, Les Murray, who suggested that an afterword be added on how the book came to be written. Thus Ella's text becomes framed in whiteness, and the ideology for this is given in the last words of Murray:

> It is good too, finally, that Mrs Simon was assisted in preparing her book by a member of one of the old settler families of our region; that would be very much in tune with Mrs Simon's own vision of how Australians should live

together in our common country. She was, after all, a relation of ours too—and it is a fact which would once have made some settler families nervous to their very great shame.

In the 1987 foreword, the point is made that things have changed and that now white Australians may rejoice in having black relations. This is supposed to be the wish of Ella Simon too; but in that discarded foreword, Professor Elkin makes the point that Ella Simon was against mixed marriages. As she recounts in her book being light-skinned meant that she was ostracised by both White and Black. She lived between two worlds and found a place in neither. Her life is somewhat similar in its isolation to Glenyse Ward in *Wandering Girl* and we may compare the quotation with which I concluded my introductory chapter with the end of Ella Simon's book:

> The old days have gone and they face a different world. They can still be proud of their Aboriginal side and make their way in today's world. Even at my age I've had to change my ways and not live in the past. But, you know, I don't think I'll ever stop wondering what I might have been . . .

Apart from the pronouns, 'they', and 'I' which signify that she sees herself as distinct from the Aboriginal people, the 'I' also serves to individualise Ella. Her life has been one of triumph over all odds and this has meant that she no longer, at least in language, identifies with her people. Who or what she identifies with may be discovered from the text. These are: (1) Christianity, (2) the Country Party and (3) a world (quoting from the cover notes of the first edition) ruled by the police. Ella Simon at the pinnacle of her life became a Justice of the Peace and an opponent of any separatist movements amongst the Blacks in her area. Her belief in the future of Aborigines in Australia is straight-forward, and this comes out when she talks about her brush with the advocates of black power:

> It was against my principles not to have a mixture of black and white. They wanted it run by Aborigines only. I just

didn't want to work under an all-Aboriginal committee, and that's the truth. I felt that this was just another colour bar. And I had the feeling that these Black Power people just wanted to get the people all to themselves. They weren't trying to assimilate them. Doing this wasn't assimilating them. It was just getting them back where they were, and I couldn't be any part of that.

Of course it would be easy to criticise the views of Ella Simon and some have done so missing the importance of those three periods of incompletion when her words break off and her story continues on in blank pages which will be filled in by other people in the later edition. When Ella Simon broke off her story, it remained incomplete and she still lived. Later, her life story would be encased and encoded as an example of an individual Black woman's success. But what I keep in mind are those three periods signifying an absence of an end to her story. When I read her book, I become aware of the depth of the wounds that assimilation cut into her mind. She writes that she was a loner and went her own way. This is apparent from her text, but she fails to delve into why she fell between two worlds and was unable to finish her story.

In my hasty classification of her book in the 'battler' genre, I was thinking white and glossed over her last words, 'but, you know, I don't think I'll ever stop wondering what I might have been . . .' which reveal a sadness at odds with the life of a 'battler' who has triumphed over adversity. It is fitting that the front and end covers of the first edition of her book show her certificate of exemption from the provisions of the Aborigines Protection Act. This was at the age of fifty-five and in 1957. In the second edition this has been deleted as if a new enlightened ideology has replaced the old. And yet escorting Ella's text before and behind like prison warders escorting a convict are white words explaining and encapsulating her. As I have stated before, a fringe minority is also an encapsulated minority.

The next book, *An Aboriginal Mother Tells of the Old and the New* by Labumore (Elsie Roughsey) was published in 1984. The text has been edited, but not so heavily as to erase all signs of her voice. It may be seen to be the female version of *Fringedweller* even to the extent that the author is allowed to tell her story in many of her own words. This gives it an immediacy and a fascination which makes it a classic in the Aboriginal life story, though it is much more than simply a life story. It is a veritable encyclopaedia of Aboriginal beliefs and practices. Elsie's suffering at the hands of the missionaries and their dormitory system which segregated Aboriginal children from their parents for the years of their childhood, is a theme running through the pages. She returns to it again and again as if trying to make sense out of the experience. As in Bob Randall's song, 'Mixed Up Man' (CAAMA cassette), she expands out from her mission experience in an effort to overcome Christian alienation. Born, bred and missionised on Mornington Island in the Gulf of Carpentaria off the far north coast of Australia, she was fortunate to remain in her own land. This allowed her identity and to accept the old ways unlike many others taken far from home and family.

In her text, we do not find a separation between *I* and *they* and moreover she often slides from objectively describing an incident to participating in it. An orality of style marks her writing, though I stress that we are not reading a transcription from a tape recording, but a written text on which Labumore carefully worked for a number of years. She is a writer and as writing is a solitary act, she acknowledges that she is a loner, though this does not affect her Aboriginality. She transcends the loneliness of the artist to write with love. She sees her life as but one among the many lives of her Lardil people, and her aim in writing her book is not to tell her story, but their story. Thus she closes her book with:

> As I close the writing of my wonderful people, I feel sad to know they are gone now. Only memories last forever.

This conclusion, symbolic as her people are still a viable community, removes Labumore's work from the battler genre and firms it as a black text. The sadness of the conclusion reminds me not only of *Fringedweller,* but also of black drama texts. It is not enough to endure as an individual or as a stagnant community. There must be movement and initiative, but the white man has taken all movement and initiative from black people. Oppression, either covert or overt, means for the oppressed only sadness. There can be no happy endings until liberation is gained.

It is only in our last book, *My Place,* by Sally Morgan that a joyful end is given to the reader. This results from a discovery of community and a fulfilment flowing in from the discovery. To exist apart from one's black community is to suffer pain and exile. Sally Morgan's book ends on this affirmative note without a further development of what it is like to be a member of an oppressed community.

In black women's writing community is felt and lived, rather than being only a matter of ideology. All three books have this sense of community, of family as theme, and *My Place* by Sally Morgan, which is close to the 'battler' genre, is a quest for family and community. She achieves her goal at the conclusion of her book and thus approaches a happy ending. But while approximating the genre, she to some extent Aboriginalises it by stepping away from her own individual life and into the lives of members of her black family. Not content with only listening to the sound of her own voice, she leaves her authorial position as the narrator of her text to let her Aboriginal family speak, but there is a further transformation back towards the 'battler' genre in the conclusion, and the text ends with these words: 'Oh, Nan,' I cried with a sudden certainty, 'I heard it too. In my heart, I heard it.'

My Place, on one level, details Sally Morgan's search for family and community. It is written in Standard English as this is her everyday discourse, but when she uses the methods of oral history to tape-record the voices of three members of her family, and introduce them into her text, the English blackens. Although the Aboriginal discourse has been edited, this in no way detracts from the authenticity of the story. In fact, it makes it more accessible to many more readers, both Black and White. As a publishing ploy, it was extremely successful and her book has sold in the tens of thousands.

All three books are examples of black women's writing in Australia. All three reflect community and family, but only *An Aboriginal Mother Tells of the Old and the New* is political in the sense that it questions the very fact of white dominance in Australia. This is seen as a catastrophe. The other two texts are accommodating and seek to remove themselves from controversy. They reflect on how things are and do not postulate any change in black/white relations in Australia; nor do they espouse any cause such as land rights, or for that matter feminism. This may be a salient signifier of urban black women's writing. Other black women's texts such as Ruby Langford's *Don't Take Your Love To Town* (1988) also steer clear of any political confrontation. The life story is concerned with the past. It details how things were, or were gained and does not challenge a future. It is only when the genre is used as a political weapon that it challenges the hegemony of White Australia.

13

Reflecting the Fringe

FRINGE FICTION OFTEN MAY BE SEEN AS AUTOBIOGRAPHICAL in that its main concern is with the special reality provided for the Aboriginal minority by the majority. Within this special frame, not only writers but each member of the minority, of the fringe, seeks to come to some sort of understanding, both of himself or herself and the reality in which they have been placed. Thus it may be seen that Aboriginal literature in Australia occupies a special place denied to the majority. If a Patrick White, a Thomas Keneally, a Dorothy Hewett decides to write about Aborigines, after they have done with them, they are discarded. The fringe after all is but a subject for their literary skills, it is not the reality which confronts them each and every day. They belong to another reality and stand outside looking into the fringe camps inhabited by the Aboriginal writer.

This does not stop white writers from declaring that their writings have an authenticity even beyond those writers of the fringe. They declare that they know the Blacks and their ways. They become upset when their friendly Blacks deny their works any authenticity, when they turn their gaze upon them and call them to account. It is then that they declare that these Aborigines have lost their culture and are not really Aborigines, that the *true* Aborigine is a gentleman, or a natural lady, whereas these ones, they belong to the fringe and should stay where they belong, away from such gentlemanly concerns as literature. Literature after all is the special area of the gentleman and gentlewoman. It arose with the middle class and even Marxist critics, the product of universities, are content to turn their gaze on what is termed high literature and ignore intrusions from the fringe or the proletariat, or use either to further their careers.

The novel is the most modern of all literary forms. Since the nineteenth century, it has reflected this modernity by becoming the most amorphous of literary genres, the most easily adapted to continually changing social and political systems, as well as being the most personal and private. With the growth of literacy, it has proved the most accessible of all literary forms; readers can escape into an artificial world. This above all may be its attraction, though poetry short and to the point would seem to be the logical choice of the fast lane. It still is the most popular form in the Aboriginal world, in the fringe where people prefer, if they have a preference, to write poetry, or listen to it—or if they write prose to incline towards the life story. Though these life stories may be received as novels in that they use fictional devices such as direct speech. A major difference is that life stories are seen as 'true', but often Aborigines when reading novels also see them as 'true'.

The fringe is still close to oral tradition, and the novel, especially the experimental novel which is the child of a literate culture is alien to it. Again the postmodern novel has drifted away from oral discourse. In extreme cases, it has become unbearable in its obscurity. Although these aberrations may be dismissed, there still remains the problem of the genre. The novel because of its origin deals with individuals, rather than with communities. Naturally, individuals in many novels are seen to make up a community, but the concerns of the individual are placed ahead of those of the community.

Novels are artefacts, ink dried into the 'staticness' of a text. Thousands upon thousands of these objects are produced each year and dumped around the world. They are consumer products, easily forgotten, and thus, perhaps we might ask, should there be any degree of enthusiasm for the arrival of the fringe novel? In a sense they may even be seen as disappointing literary products, lacking the vigor of the new Aboriginal poetry. The acclaim which greeted the arrival of the first of these novels: 'If I wore a hat, I'd take it off to Colin Johnson for his brilliant first novel, *Wildcat Falling*,' may be queried. Is this acclaim accorded to the exotic novelty of a novel, a cultural artefact of Europe, being produced by an Aborigine? Is this acclaim a cry of wonder at an Aborigine managing to do such a thing?

A cry of wonder was part of the response; but then, these novels are seen as challenges to the society which allows conditions to produce the kind of characters depicted; as showing the bond between earth and man, the flux and reflux of life and death and the encounter of black people with white society. Thus they have a social value. Moreover, these novels by being written in a realist mode allow themselves to be read as social texts. This aspect was stressed until recently by prefaces and forewords which urged the reader to read them as sociological tracts. An assumption being that the said reader would be White.

The first works of Aboriginal prose appeared in various states of disguise. These were folklore, or illustrations to anthropological works, adaptions of myths, or rewritten autobiography. The first novel written by an Aborigine, *Wildcat Falling* (1965), was described as semi-autobiographical as was the second, *Karobran* (1978). The lives of the principal characters of these two novels depict the personal dilemma of being Aboriginal in Australia. This determines their fate, and gives them a degree of tragic inevitability which is close to the tragic classicism of Ancient Greece. The inevitability of encountering violence, unfairness, poverty, the squashing of aspirations, denial of beauty, ridicule and lack of freedom to determine one's own fate is as close to a reliance on divine inevitabilities as can be found in modern fiction.

Aboriginality, or Blackness may be seen as a variant of fate, the condition which determines and predicates the actions of the characters; but this 'fate' is not so much individual, as collective. Young Aboriginal men and women, at the crossroads of their lives, reflect on the dispossession, on the denial by white society. They go up against fate, against their own Aboriginality or Blackness, and either achieve some catharsis, or go under. In a sense these novels seek to remain close to reality, without excluding the symbolic, so that their message may not be lost.

It is rare to find in Aboriginal novels any trace of contemporary European innovations in structure and style, and little attempt to utilise Aboriginal oral narrative structures. In my latest fictional work *Doin Wildcat, A Novel Koori Script* (1988) I do attempt to escape from the genre by using Aboriginal English throughout and by refusing to have a happy ending, or an ending in itself. However I do not try to go beyond realist conventions, but try to faithfully mirror the Aboriginal condition. It is difficult to escape realism and doubtful if an attempt is worthwhile. In fact one of the latest novels published, *Women of the Sun* (1985), is a classic realist text journalistic in its prose. It seeks to mirror the continuing Aboriginal experience in the State of Victoria over the last 150 odd years, and does this in a style far removed from Aboriginal prose narrative styles. The historical novel, *Pemulwuy, the Rainbow Warrior* (1987), by Eric Willmot, has some sentences and individual words from the Sydney area, but the author does not seek to re-create an original syntax in English for his Aboriginal characters.

It may be asked: Is there a definable fringe novel? Or are there just Australian novelists writing with a darker shade of pale? By this, I mean, are these just writers who have adopted the form of the novel as the means of their literary expression—one capable of reaching the widest readership—or do they try to get over an Aboriginal point of view in content and language.

First of all, it is difficult to divorce these texts from Australia. The fringe novels so far published are set in Tasmania, Victoria, Western Australia and New South Wales. It must be pointed out here that I am writing about less than a dozen novels, or long fictional works, three of them set exclusively in the mid twentieth century, two spanning the time from the Invasion to the present, and two set in the early stages of the Invasion. The dealing with past and present is in itself an Aboriginal trait in that Aborigines are very conscious of their history. They, as do many other indigenous peoples, look for solutions in the past rather than in the future, then seek to recapture it symbolically in words. In traditional society, the past, the remote dreaming past, spilt over into the present and served to shape the future. The past age of heroic ancestral beings was the template to which present and future Aboriginal society had to conform, and this looking back on the past is still with us, though our heroes have changed to those like Pemulwuy and Tjandamara.

Often in these novels when white people appear, they are conventionalised, for example in the historical novels we have the white evil in opposition to the black good. Aboriginal writers are very conscious that history is a white construct in that a past *truth* is maintained, and are eager to redress the balance. In a sense when we talk of history we are talking of *myth* masquerading as objective history, and thus the so-called *real* people are not as important as the universal, or archetypes which are called upon by the present day writer. In this sense Captain Cook is as much an archetypal figure as Pemulwuy and archetypal figures are best dealt with in the novel which does not masquerade as truth.

The idea of an objective past being important simply because it is the past, has really no bearing on Aboriginality, but myth has! Myth is a retelling of what is seen as the past, but a past pregnant with present meaning. Thus in my novel, *Long Live Sandawara* (1979), it is not the past fact of Sandawara's suffering that is important, but the fact that he is an archetype spilling over to influence the present. The presence of myth may be easily recognised in that often causal relationships depend on supernatural or above normal powers. In *Women of the Sun* (1983), as script, the mythic dimensions of the story are emphasised by the poems of the author. These poems integral to the whole disappear when the script becomes video tape and then novel. It is legitimate to ask why this has happened.

James Ricketson, the director of the video series, in his

introduction to the first part of *Women of the Sun*, as script, writes:

> I fell in love immediately with Episode One, 'Alinta—The Flame' read it twice and made copious notes of changes in the script that I thought might be necessary. Although the story was wonderful I felt that the white characters suffered the same fate that many female characters suffer in Australian films and plays—they were two-dimensional. They were thoroughly nasty, insensitive men with no redeeming qualities whatsoever. Quite apart from my disbelief that characters such as these would have no better side to them, it made no dramatic sense.

Words are not innocent creatures, or do they only have a single meaning? A careful reading often brings out a hidden meaning. In this case, the director is saying that he wanted a product made on his terms. He thus subverted the Aboriginality of the text and most of its mythic elements were removed. Eventually, when a novel was constructed from this 'award-winning TV series' it was a simple realist novel, a consumer product similar to other products of its type.

If I examine each stage of the *Women of the Sun*, from script to novel, what I see is a lessening of Aboriginality so that by the time we reach the novel all that remains is a nice story of the sad-but-true genre. I might, if I am so inclined, even read in the progression a lessening of Aboriginal control. By the time the novel is reached the Aboriginality is so diluted that there is no need for an apology for the supposed weakness of the genre.

Genres have developed as a European way of categorising works of literature. In themselves, they are ways of manipulating the text so that the reader is led from an intuitive to a logical response to the work. Not only this, but the Aboriginal writer is led to believe that there are fixed categories of literature to which he or she must conform. If we as writers accept this we, in effect, dilute the Aboriginality of our work. If we consider ourselves as existing in an Aboriginal cultural matrix, then we must know that part of our culture lies outside European conventions.

It is precisely this part, this Aboriginality that is missed by the European editor who because he or she belongs to another culture finds it wrong to construct a narrative prose work (a novel or life story) according to an unfamiliar structure. There is a right (read, 'European') way of doing things and so the work must be edited towards this. Ricketson, ignoring all the stereotyping which is a feature of Anglo-Celtic Australian literature, finds this unbelievable in an Aboriginal work, though it is part of the special quality of existence in the fringe that often all evils are accepted as coming from the European.

These Europeans, for example, assume an archetypal role of evil incarnate as in my novel *Dr Wooreddy's Prescription for Enduring the Ending of the World* (1983). They are considered to be evil and as evil is banal, their banality is brought out by stereotyping. If the reader can accept that there is a mythic structure lying at the bottom of some Aboriginal texts, then what is read is a simple binary opposition of the white-evil opposed to the black-good.

In both *Women of the Sun* (as script) and *Dr Wooreddy* mythic elements are present from the beginning. Hyllus Maris is explicit in giving a mythic cast to her script by beginning with a poem setting her story in a context from the first dawn. *Dr Wooreddy* also stresses myth in establishing an opposition between sea-as-evil and land-as-good, with the num (Europeans) as part of that sea-evil. The main character experiences their arrival as a supernatural event, and the first chapter unfolds within a structure of oppositions, good (child as innocence) seeing evil (European ships), and extending further into the moral good of traditional society opposed to the evils of the European convict system brought to Tasmania. This opposition is seen also in *Women of the Sun*. Europeans intrude into the pristine world of Australia as an evil disrupting force.

A close reading of Aboriginal texts often reverses our opinion of genre classification. This may appear contradictory, but it is precisely these points which are picked up by Aborigines. As Bruce McGuinness, in *Aboriginal Writing Today*, says:

> When Aboriginal people write they write in a style. They're able to adapt various styles of writing so that what they want

to write about is there. It's hidden. It's contained within their writing, if one can go through the subterfuge, the camouflage that they use when they're writing.

And so in the three novels dealing with the past, fantasy, mystery and the supernatural appear to point away from any simple realist interpretation. These may be absent in the novels set in the recent past, but if they are, they are replaced by patterns of moods, feelings and intuitions.

The recognition of Aboriginal reality as stemming from the Dreaming or Dreamtime is explicit or implicit and is a trait of Aboriginality in these novels. A state, either mental or mythical, lies underneath the ordinary day-to-day consciousness of the Aboriginal character, which sometimes erupts to give certain passages a surreal quality. This again contradicts a first facile reading which sees these texts as simply realist, naturalist, or social realist. This recognition of an atemporal state in itself leads to mixed genre.

Aboriginal reality exists uneasily with European reality: the Dreamtime with clocktime. This is best seen in Bob Bropho's *Fringedweller*, in which it is impossible to establish a correct chronology of events. The underlying reality is the Dreamtime into which whitefella time intrudes with fixed dates. It is as if clocktime emerged out of the Dreamtime, only to fall back into it. This is found also in Bobby Merritt's *The Cake Man* at the beginning of the drama which begins with archetypes before reforming as a naturalist text which endures for a time until towards the end where the audience, or reader is confronted by a black man suddenly erupting out of the play and speaking to them about 'two realities'. In Lionel Fogarty's verse, time is even more disrupted in the deliberate misuse of verb tenses. Tenses are ideological in that they mark out the time model used by a particular language group, and when two language groups collide there are grammatical problems reflecting the collision of different ideologies.

The problem of time collision is seen in *Wildcat Falling* in which tenses are used to mark out time segments in a way used in Aboriginal oral narrative. Although the text has been heavily edited, the tenses are used creatively in that past and present do not refer to the narrative present or past scenes, but switch when the mood demands. Thus sometimes the past is presented in the past tense, and at other times it is presented in the present tense. In *Long Live Sandawara* time is presented in a rather complicated manner in that two pasts collide through an old man into a present where day and night is reversed in that the characters live through the night and sleep through the day. When they do seek a reversal into normal or whitefella time, tragedy occurs.

Irony and humour are used often in Aboriginal novels to lessen the reality of the narrative, to bring into question the fact that the novel is supposed to be mirroring reality, but that to use a white form as the mirror is to invite failure. Irony and humour is used to drop the reader out of the story and into the mind of the novelist, as towards the end of *Long Live Sandawara* where the white character, Ron, suddenly becomes aware that the story is ending and with it his supposed reality. The reader is lifted out of the story with the comment:

> '. . . something terrible like the last few pages of a good story
> flickering to a tragic end and the sudden awareness of the
> reader that soon he will be alone again.'

Aboriginal novels are never escapist fiction. There are no adventures recounted for the sake of, for the pleasure of unravelling a plot. They are overtly partisan and consciously committed to either explaining the Aboriginal people to themselves or to a wider European readership. What marks them out is that the main character is an Aborigine and surrounded with the problems with which we began this chapter.

The first Aboriginal novel to be published was *Wildcat Falling*. Written in the early sixties, it comes complete with the usual foreword by a white person. This introduction in effect questions the Aboriginality of the text and we are justified in seeing it as flawed; but, although the main character is extremely individualised, though without the identification of a name, he has been accepted by other Aborigines as being a symbol of those light-skinned Aborigines of his time who sought to evade their fate by hiding beneath the coloured carpet of other races in better standing with Europeans. This may be contrasted with Sally Morgan in her life story, *My Place*, in which she grows up thinking she is Indian.

Briefly the novel concerns an unnamed character who is released from jail into the white world. He wanders around for a few days and ends up back inside. It is written in first person, though this 'I' is uneasy and the character often exchanges it for third person. There is a strong sense of anomie in the novel, and an opposition between Aboriginal and white society, in the space between which the character drifts. Only one other Aboriginal character, an old man, has any strength, and he is a symbol of the character's inner Aboriginality with which he is seeking to identify. His story, or life is similar to Aboriginal growth in the West. Institutionalisation at an early age; an attachment to mother; life in an Aboriginal fringe camp; alcohol; and a strong sense of his Aboriginality which will not let him rest. The story ends with a flight into the bush, an aspect of Aboriginal fiction in that the bush is always seen as a friend and is often contrasted with the enemy of the city. This is also an important element in the later novel, *The Day of the Dog*, by Archie Weller.

In 1988, I returned to the story again in *Doin Wildcat*. The character had gone to gaol, written *Wildcat Falling* in gaol as a project of rehabilitation, been released and much later was hired to script his novel. *Doin Wildcat* is on one level the story of the making of the film. On another level it shows what happens to the Aboriginality of a script when it is made into a film by a white director. A third level is to try and escape the conventions of the novel. Conventions such as an ending. Also it was an attempt to write an entire fictional work in dialect and to include some examples of contemporary Aboriginal oral literature. All in all, I consider it my best work to date; others consider it my worst.

The second novel to be written by an Aborigine, though only published in 1978, is *Karobran*, by Monica Clare. It too is assumed to be autobiographical, though written in the third person and with a main character named Isabella. The narrative is straightforward in a realistic mode and is framed by a publisher's note, foreword, preface and introduction—which seems very heavy for a slim volume of ninety-five pages. The text itself has been heavily compromised by the editing of Jack Horner and others. This may account for the social realist tone of the finished product, though at least such motifs as the land as refuge, the problem of alcohol, institutionalisation, the basic structural opposition between Black and White are allowed to remain. Still, the oppositions are resolved in a socialist-type synthesis. What is lacking is irony and humour (as opposed to good-humour) which I would expect to find in an Aboriginal novel. The style of the edited product is bland, and it would be interesting to compare it with the original manuscript.

My second novel, *Long Live Sandawara* appeared in 1979. It has a split structure in which the present is set off against a heroic past of Aboriginal resistance. In the past segments, I wrote in an element of mysticism in that Sandawara is seen as a mapan, magician or trickster. This is in keeping with the oral account as found in the Kimberley. The *mapan*, or trickster also appears in many of the stories of Paddy Roe and may be seen as a traditional character of Aboriginal narrative. Sandawara is set off by the present day character, the urban youth, Alan. A link between past and present is provided by the old man, Noorak, who tells Alan about Sandawara and eventually takes him North.

I have been criticised for making Sandawara, based on the historical Tjandamara, into a heroic character. I did this because most Aborigines are familiar with westerns and can accept such a hero, then the novel as genre lends itself to the creation of the heroic. If one wishes to write a novel, one must accept the conventional structure, or it is no longer a novel. This is a reason why I called *Doin Wildcat* a novel Koori script as I felt that it lay outside the genre.

The Day of the Dog by Archie Weller was published in 1981. It is set in Perth and is similar to *Wildcat*

Falling in that it begins with the release from prison of an Aboriginal man, though he is named (Dougie Dooligan). The rest of the novel is taken up with his adventures which are structured towards his fate. He is shot a few days after he is released. Archie Weller has stated that the story is based on true facts and so it may also be seen as autobiographical or biographical.

Archie Weller is an accomplished writer of both short stories and novels, but I find his narrative style different from Aboriginal discourse in that it is poetic or flowery, though this does not detract from the story, and the authenticity of the Nyoongah voice is heard in the dialogue. The novel is realist and linear in time. There is the familiar theme of the bush as refuge, but this time, the urban Nyoongahs reveal their alienation from its healing powers.

Archie Weller is one of the new generation of writers, an urban generation, thus he might be showing that with the arrival of a generation who have known nothing but city life, there is a lack of land awareness and a growing lumpenproletarianisation. City Aborigines are moving away from their sense of community and are becoming a class with the poorer Whites on the bottom strata of society. This progression is found also in *The First Born*, a trilogy of plays by Jack Davis. The dramas chart the generations of an Aboriginal family from the thirties to the present. Aboriginal culture becomes less and less with each succeeding generation until finally in the last play of the trilogy, *Barungin*, there is little difference between black and white lifestyles.

Archie Weller documents this decay in his work and seeks to reverse the trend. In his novel, the strong power of the earth is a potent force emerging to pervade important parts of his novel with a sense of Aboriginality, even though his characters refuse to accept their affinity with it:

> The youths revel in the hard work and in each other's company. They have not been together just by themselves for a long time. Amidst the tortured screams of the dying trees, as the chainsaw's teeth bite into their virgin bodies, and the rumbling of the old faded red dozer smashing into the trees,

knocking them senseless, and pushing them into broken piles,
their raw yellow roots jagging obscenely into the air, and the
thudding of the cruel axe—amidst all this Doug no longer
needs the friendship of the bush. In all its silent dignity it
draws away from the youth who so badly needed a proper
friend. Now he laughs as he slaughters the trees with his
companions.

In this passage Aboriginal reality is seen to sweep away the
realist mode, though some readers may identify here the
'pathetic fallacy': the ascribing of human feelings and
attributes to nature; but it is more than this. Nature to the
Aborigine, is a living, breathing sentience, and such an
attitude may be seen in other works of Aboriginal literature,
for example in *Wildcat Falling* where the bush becomes
friendly to the main character.

*Dr Wooreddy's Prescription for Enduring the Ending of
the World*, published in 1983, has already been discussed in
some detail. Briefly the novel purports to record the life
story of Wooreddy, the husband of Truganini, the so-called
last of the Tasmanians. The narrative discourse is straight
and linear, from childhood to death, though there are
aspects of Aboriginality throughout, and on a deeper level
the novel may be read as an account of Wooreddy's spiritual
life, rather than a facile rendition of the genocide of the
Tasmanian people. Both readings are possible, and the
ending is symbolic in that when Wooreddy dies his spirit
ascends into the sky to become part of the Aboriginal flag.
By this I mean to imply that Wooreddy lives on forever in
his community and is a source of strength to them.

I have already discussed aspects of the script of *Women of
the Sun* by Hyllus Maris, and the novel is a spin-off from
the video series. It holds a contradiction in that on the front
of the cover it is described as a novel and as a quartet of
stories on the back. It may be seen as both. Each story leads
into the next and the four different female characters may
be seen as the same incarnating spirit, or if this is not
accepted, as the symbolic *Aboriginal woman*. The text is
naturalistic and chronicles the history of the Koori people
of Victoria as suffered by the women. The modern segment

parallels *Karobran* in treatment and subject matter. In *Women of the Sun* there is little of the violence and harshness found in the novels of male writers.

Pemulwuy, the Rainbow Warrior by Eric Willmot (1987) is a conventional novel purporting to set the record straight about the first invasion of the British at Port Jackson and the resulting contact and resistance in the area. It is very descriptive and the black characters act like Europeans. It is difficult to know what to make of it. What seems to have been lost is the idea that there were two cultures and peoples in conflict. Pemulwuy conducts his resistance movement like a British general. For all this, it is interesting reading and has been well researched, which may be the reason why I find the prose stilted. If not for the narrative structure of the text, it might have been a history book. In fact not only are maps and background material provided, but also a page of references.

I see the novel as being essentially fiction and find such documentation unnecessary. But this book because it purports to tell the 'truth' about historical events, needs such a non-fictional frame to defend itself against falsity. This urge to tell the truth through fictional or dramatic gestures is seen in other texts such as Jack Davis' *Kullark* and *The Dreamers*. What we are dealing with may be described as documentary fiction, or literature with a message or a 'truth' which may be proved by recourse to reference works. It is 'commitment' with a vengeance.

14

Centring the Fringe

The National Aboriginal & Islander Observance Day Committee (NAIDOC) Poster for 1988 held the blurred three-dimensional face of a young Aboriginal child, a signifier of peace. The slogan beneath read: 'Recognise and Share the Survival of the Oldest Culture in the World'. In a year of white celebration supposedly boycotted by Aborigines the message was clear. The Aborigines wanted their place in a multicultural Australia and separatism was seen as not a valid alternative. This poster provides evidence that the Aborigines are indeed entering a post-activist phase, and representatives of Aboriginal literature such as Jack Davis and Oodgeroo Noonuccal instead of boycotting or ignoring the festivities of 1988 participated in events which might be construed as part of the year long celebration.

1988 in many ways was the year of bribing the Aborigine. Aboriginal culture was invited into the centre. Art galleries had exhibitions of Aboriginal art; theatres put on Aboriginal plays, and a number of books were published, most of them in cooperation with white editors. Even in bicentennial celebrations Aboriginal participation was evident. Some Aboriginal groups pressed for a boycotting of any and all celebrations, but the call went unheeded. Oodgeroo Noonuccal wrote a special piece for the World Exposition in Brisbane and Jack Davis brought his play *Barungin* there as a fringe cultural event. The President of the Australian Institute of Aboriginal Studies, a Nyoongah and also a writer, gave the Wentworth Lecture for 1988. It was an important paper separating what he called 'land rites' from 'land rights'. This might have become a focus of debate in Aboriginal political circles, but few of the media activists took up the challenge. They continued to mouth well-worn slogans and organise street marches which, if they were exciting events in themselves, failed to generate any new political initiatives. The activists indeed moved away from political confrontation and centred their efforts on publicising Aboriginal culture. Thus, Aboriginal dance groups led the main street march in Sydney on Australia Day.

Someone might now ask what has this got to do with Aboriginal literature? Many Aboriginal writers have been activists and still are. Their works are examples of 'committed' literature, and call for action. This action has not been forthcoming and literature may be seen as simply a form of symbolic protest. In fact with Oodgeroo Noonuccal's participation in one of the main, though unofficial highlights of the Bicentennial year, this 'commitment' itself may be called in doubt. But in times of inactivity, what better thing for a writer to do than to write.

I must conclude this book and I would like to end it with an analysis of a piece I wrote for the bicentennial celebrations of 1988. I too participated in my own way. I know that in orthodox books, I should draw all the strands of discussion into a neat conclusion, but in Aboriginal affairs there are no neat conclusions, or happy endings at least for the moment.

Firstly, I would like to start off with creative writing itself. I start here, at the root, because so much bullshit has been put forth on this subject, usually from a Western perspective beginning with the ego existing in splendid solitude and from this divine monad coming the great work. I, instead of seeing the ego as splendidly isolated, see it as being social, that is man or woman is a social being and that the ego of man or woman is not only formed by society or by the community, but extends out from the head or beyond the skin, the bark, to thrust back into the community.

There is really no inner or outer isolation, and the tree of the ego is swayed and moved more by what is happening around, the breezes, the earth, the touching hands of a human being, than by say the sap rising from the roots and up the trunk and permeating each branch, twig and leaf. Naturally, if we did concentrate on the inner sap of the tree, its essence so to speak, we would find that it too is determined by outer things, the soil and its content, the rain, or moisture and so on. So it seems that this isolation, sometimes put out as being the abode of the writer and his ego, this splendid isolation is an illusion or, if you want, a man-made construct.

In beginning the analysis of a piece of my own writing, I would like to quote from the French theorist, Roland Barthes ('The Death of the Author', in *Image-Music-Text*):

> . . . that a text is not a line of words releasing a single
> 'theological' meaning (the 'message' of the Author — God) but
> a multi-dimensional space in which a variety of writings,
> none of them original, blend and clash. The text is a tissue of
> quotations drawn from the innumerable centres of cultures.

This quotation should be kept in mind. Now first of all perhaps what all of us in Australia have been getting in this past year of 1988 is 'Celebration of a Nation', which has two distinct meanings, or significations to what may be broadly separated into the two centres of culture in Australia: The European — specifically, the Anglo-Celtic — and the Aboriginal.

Now these are not two binary oppositions, separate and distinct, but spill over into each other, for example a reading of a map of any suburb in a typical Australian city, for example Brisbane, shows an intermixture of these two cultures. Street names, road names, for example: Burbong Road. 'Burbong' is a signifier of Aboriginality; 'road', of Europeanness, and if we extend this further both constitute a signifier of Australianness, and in a deeper reading may extend into the superstructure of Australian society to reveal the overall position of Europeans and Aborigines, for in Burbong Road few Aborigines live, there are few signs of Aborigines, the roadside is divided into blocks holding

European houses and so on. There is a marked absence of Aboriginality in the area except for that name, and perhaps a few names of houses, or intersecting roads. The indigenous people have gone away leaving only isolated words of their language to signify their absence.

Now, I turn to my written text, rather than the text of a map, or the text of a suburb, though we must remain aware that any system of signs form a text which may be read, and by reading I mean only the deciphering as much as we are able to of a system of signs.

CELEBRATION OF A NATION

Cockatoo folds down to the ground beside a tall broken-trunk tree emptied out by a long ago bushfire. Dark interior gleams in soft morning light breaking it wide open into the cubed edging of wood turned charcoal in that long ago fire, in that long ago burning into hollow log formed for this occasion, for cockatoo, yellow-sulphur crest, seeking to ignite that flame, to excavate that hollow, to fill it with the broken honeycomb of bones pulverised into broken cells oozing with honey, dripping with honey from the far north as a cry resounds, hoarsely like the craw-crawling of crow biding his time, but missing his time as cockatoo takes the sound and unfolds, stealing the air with white wings as he circles in a heavy lazy floating of hot wings, once, twice and up into a green tree not too far away and green-lush with the hot sun baking earth brown, waiting for the gift of the north in that hoarse cry, that crow-call clawing at the fire bubbling with the blackened heavy drum filled water brown with the swirl of leaking tea stains, swirling with leaves edging into the hot morning, reaching out a smell to cockatoo residing with this caravan, this righteous camp of souls urging hope regained in the ceremony. But the call comes again, clawing through to where Cookalingee dances her mock dance of despair in a show revealing death and survival, life and hope all suited-up and short-panted for a new dawn to commence.

Cookalingee, lithe young dancing body evading hard masculinity of occasion by partnering a chair. Inert fissures

performing less a hopeful change than the eroded squares of
charcoal fashioned fully for this occasion as Cookalingee
whirls out her female dance of unable to endure yet enduring
this time of mourning, this time of sadness, this time of
celebration of youthful litheful dancer's body enduring a
swirling of the air, of atonement, of past meals being prepared
and discarded with no thought of this latter day engraved in
the motions of her body encircling the chair, thrusting motion
towards, receiving it back. Her dress fluttering, her hair
fluttering, her arms eroding the urgency of cook house fire.
Her energy, her youth seeking to engulf that chair. Heavy
inertness, less than the tree charcoal under the hot sun of
voices preparing bodies for the ceremony. Cookalingee
sinking down in a crying at her lot, in a crying at the lot of
her people responding to the calling, crow-calling, craw-
crawling from that camp site far from her dreaming place
where now feet stamp out an encircled belief around the
stillness of the body waiting for honeyed tree, crushed-bone
tree, life-long tree oozing with honey dripping from the
ruptured body cells.

Far north homeland green with many urgencies of plants
flows down and withers into dry yellow dusks and air drained
of moisture and life-giving ceremonies such as this being
stamped out, performed sacred and entire, secret and
meaningful beyond clicking camera booms and pens
whispering words into black boxes rearranging magnetic
particles to record unknown records. Feet stamping, knees
bending thudding the feet down, thudding the feet down.
Pow, pow, puffs of dust rising, lingering on the crow call.
Cockatoo watching safe in his near but far away tree as
Cookalingee suffers her fate without knowing that she is
suffering her fate in the dance, of feet thudding up particles of
dust to manacle the magnetic rearrangement of the atoms into
an American voice questioning: 'Say, why do you think it's
called Bennelong Point anyway?': To manacle the magnetic
arrangement of the atoms into an American voice replying:
'Guess, because it's bin a long time since they owned it'.

And as the feet thud, and as a dancer stops to catch a still
position on one thin black leg, then gives a quick convulsion
simmering into discontent a black queen in a white queen's

paraphernalia of long white gloves extruding to the elbow a nasalised unhoneyed voice duly commanding a royal performance of the particles to cease, then start again in ordered lines of: 'My loyal subjects and all de men. I range over your faces and recall your pleasing vanities in selecting my husband and my royal self to be here, thus evading any unpleasantries in not only not being at home, but in being here in a somewhat darkened form, though smeared with the whiteness of my gloves as befitting the occasion dealing with the smearing of pipe clay somewhat resembling the sails of flocks of cockatoos circling overhead and tugging at dark bodies, sublime and horizontal of these my first ships touching these, our shores with the rotten hulks of despair and future crime. Do I hear the craw-crawling of crow, is that the screeching of vivid livid sails? Sulphurous fumes decorate our heads. Our diadem glitters with the calling eyes of this, our day of mourning being celebrated in our subject, Cookalingee's dance. God bless her female heart and dishpan hands. Her warm body and subdued meant-for-better-things mind. It's in the gloves, the white gloves, cockatoo's crest, and the craw-crawling of our subject, crow. Let them dance, coffin awaits them—but, but before then, a pause, a pause, magnetic particles record, this our refrain:

> A youthman was found hanging in his cell
> On this our day, when everywhere the Aborigines
> Were dancing, everywhere the Aborigines were marching.
> They're just like us, is our quaint refrain,
> They like balls and footy and songs and beer:
> We ignore their call for Landrights!

> On Australia's day, a youthman strangled in a cell:
> Who killed him; who were his murderers?
> Not I, said the cop, I only took him in.
> Not I, said this town, I never spoke his name,
> It's no fault of mine that he has to die—
> We treat them as we do our own,
> There's no racism in our town.

> On this, our day a youthman dies while his people
> Camp nearby trying to recover stolen land.

They daub this town with white and raise high
The Red, the Black and Gold.
The red is his blood,
The black his skin,
The gold our cause as bright as sun:
We want our land and there is no turning back.

A waving wink of a hand behind a smile as the ceremony
continues with black bodies and faces gleaming behind the
stains of white clay mourning the absence of ceremony at the
site burdened with the tree excavated by the sulphurous crest
of cockatoo lifting a gnarled claw to scratch out the rhythm of
clapsticks calling him away from pursuing didgeridoo
droning out his place in the proceedings as Cookalingee gives
a swirl light years away from the heavy stamp of heels
scattering the dust particles and arousing the bees to spread
out in a thick line of nectar-laden flight as the bones are
crushed, hu, hu, hu, hu, into honeycomb slices as
Cookalingee slinks down embracing her beloved chair heavy
and inert, slippery with the scented sweating polish of her
limbs aching and clutching in mourning the rounded body of
the tree trunk, light and grey and quivering with the heated
air as didgeridoo squawks cockatoo into a belated arrival of
folding down right on the very ragged, blackened splinter of
poor, fella tree: him gone along with that fella; him dead one
now; him honey one now; him honeycomb now; him
secreting the sweetness of Cookalingee—she little one, one
time big with her hollow tree trunk filled with honeycomb,
filled with honeycomb, sweet sap honey dripping. Her son,
him bin hanged in that jail. Him bin died in that jail cell just
yesterday time. Bub, buh, buh, buh, buh—didgeridoo calling
crow lounging as Cookalingee stirs her loins all atremble to
make the magnetic particles align themselves again
American-wise.
   'Say, what is this? Is this what you call a corroboree? Hey,
you guys, this is a dinkum corroboree! And we can stay? And
we can take pictures? Say, our folks back home will just love
this!'
   WARU, WARU! Attention, attention! Hey, hey,
Cookalingee leaping to the rhythm of Warumpi Band
dissipating the cries from the past. Cockatoo screeches the last

of his didgeridoo sounds. Tree quivers and becomes inert as the bones are laid to rest and the white clay soothes his sulphurous wounds and makes him whole enough for the bees to enter through his skull and plaster his insides with wax dripping with the yellow nectar of their flight. WARU, WARU, clak-crak, clak-crak, clak-crak, clak—measured rhythm of clap-sticks falter into syncopation. Mourn-ing, mourn-ing, mourn-ing, didgeridoo murmurs before picking up on the rhythm, cel-e-bration, cel-e-bration, cel-e-bration. And their skins shine darkly under the full sun light and their skins shine whitely in the full sunlight as their bodies dance to cel-e-bration, cel-e-bration, cel-e-bration; ofa, ofa, ofa, ofa; nat shun, nat shun, nat shun—shunit, shunit, shunit, shunit . . .

Now what are we, as readers, to make of my first paragraph rather long and bereft of city signs? How are we to read it? Cockatoo is but a bird, or is he, and what is his relationship to the hollow tree, to fire?

How are we to take this bird? How are we to take his role? If we seek to come to grips with this sign, it breaks open into an icon, as in the Macintosh computer, and this icon is symbol. Cockatoo as symbol. A blonde-haired white man with all that that entails for an Aborigine, but further, if we take into account Barthes' quotation in which he sees the text as multi-dimensional coming from numerous centres of culture; if we know that this piece of writing, this text is from an Aborigine we might look beyond the obvious, go into the icon to elicit further meanings.

We must remain aware of the intertextuality of the text, and of the centre of Aboriginal culture, specifically localised here as northern. And again if we are or have been aware of the events of January, 1988, 'Celebration of a Nation', and of the caravan of people, traditional Aboriginal people travelling down to Sydney, this will make us consider that our icons may owe a great deal to Arnhem Land Culture, and again with the Aboriginal view of the celebration as being a celebration of survival, of an escape from genocidal practices added to media reports of an old man dying on the way to Sydney and ceremonies being conducted, we might make the connection that cockatoo is a bird associated with the funeral services in Arnhem Land, and if we know of the Djambidj cycle of ceremonies, we will be aware of this.

Cockatoo is connected with funeral ceremonies and in our text this is brought out by a further icon of the hollow log, or hollow tree, and pulverised bones, referring to the method of finally laying to rest the deceased in Arnhem Land. Another icon in the text is 'crow', again a bird interested in everything about death. Crow is a bird who is familiar with death. He is always close to it, whereas cockatoo manages to keep his distance. Other icons remain to be deciphered, but I leave these with the comment that the caravan refers to the people travelling down from the north with their ceremonies to fertilise what they see as a land barren of Aboriginality. I stress that I am not so much interested in whether this is true or not, but it is an ideological position held by people in Arnhem Land.

The last sentence of the paragraph introduces an icon as a character: *Cookalingee*. Here, there is a shift in that the traditional symbols or icons give way to one signifying Urban Aboriginal culture. The icon infolds a poem of Oodgeroo's, *Cookalingee*, and the sign is meant to signify her poem and all that it contains, plus more, but I'll get to that. First, I'll give Oodgeroo's poem.

COOKALINGEE (For Elsie Lewis)

Cookalingee, now all day
Station cook in white man's way,
Dressed and fed, provided for,
Sees outside her kitchen door
Ragged band of her own race,
Hungry nomads, black of face.
Never begging, they stand by,
Silent, waiting, wild and shy,
For they know that in their need
Cookalingee give them feed.
Peering in, their deep dark eyes
Stare at stove with wide surprise,
Pots and pans and kitchen-ware,
All the white-man wonders there.

Cookalingee, lubra still
Spite of white-man station drill,
Knows the tribal laws of old:
'Share with others what you hold';
Hears the age-old racial call:
'What we have belongs to all.'
Now she gives with generous hand
White man tucker to that band,
Full tin plate and pannikin
To each hunter, child and gin.
Joyful, on the ground they sit,
With only hands for eating it.
Then upon their way they fare,
Bellies full and no more care.

Cookalingee, lubra still,
Feels her dark eyes softly fill,
Watching as they go content,
Natural as nature meant.
And for all her place and pay
Is she happy now as they?
Wistfully she muses on
Something bartered, something gone.
Songs of old days,
The walkabout, the old free ways.
Blessed with everything she prized,
Trained and safe and civilized,
Much she has that they have not,
But is hers the happier lot?

Lonely in her paradise
Cookalingee sits and cries.

Oodgeroo of the Tribe Noonuccal
(formerly Kath Walker)

There is one *last* thing to add about the final words of my first paragraph. These, 'a new dawn to commence' signifies Oodgeroo's second book of poetry: *The Dawn Is At Hand* (Brisbane, 1966).

Cookalingee signifies urban culture, modern dance as opposed to traditional dance. The chair signifies dead wood, a manufactured article. Sydney or any city with its hardness of man-madeness: roads, and buildings, cars and life itself. But she is an Aborigine, and as she dances her city dance, the crow calls her to the camp site where the people from the north are conducting proper ceremonies. In Aboriginal dance, the feet stamp; in European dance, feet are but points and dancing appears to be an attempt to evade the solidity of gravity.

The third paragraph refers back to the camp site and the ceremony revitalising the south. Urban and country come together. The reporters and television crews that accompanied the caravan are referred to and encapsulated in Cockatoo in his near but far away tree. They are separated from the ceremony by not having the cultural knowledge from the Aboriginal centre. This is stressed by the American voices. Outside participants, though not unsympathetic, they cannot read the obvious, cannot connect signifier and signified into sign.

The ceremony is magical, is Aboriginal, and evokes a white response, strange and as distant to many people as the ceremonies of Aborigines are. Directly, it is an intrusion, or a fragment of intertextuality, from Jean Genet's, *The Blacks*; indirectly, it may refer, or be a referent to Roland Barthes' quotation. Death enters directly in a welter of icons or symbols, as the Drag Queen gives a version of the celebration and the invasion of Australia from black and white perspectives. It is her/his right as a complex icon. Beyond blackness and whiteness, beyond maleness and femaleness, partaking of both, and of both, and of the original crime, and as perpetrator and victim, he/she reiterates present crime and death.

The poem she/he recites is from my collection: *The Song Circle of Jacky* (1986). The central stanza is built around the children's rhyme, 'Who Killed Cock Robin', which has been used for a number of folk songs including 'Who Killed Norma Jean' by Pete Seeger, and as such folk songs signify music in good standing with the Left, we have another icon or sign signifying the alliance, or support of the Aboriginal cause by the Left. Nothing is simple it seems, though the last stanza is made up of direct signs signifying the meaning of the colours of the Aboriginal flag, though personalised in an individual dying a jail death.

The colour *white* as white pipe clay, or ash signifies mourning, a time of mourning, or in mourning. White in this text signifies this, among other things, for as I have said signs are icons which are symbol things. They are complexities which may be broken down or built up just as texts may be built up or broken down. The perceiving of these signs is an act of reading with a reader who brings his own readability to the sign and the sign-system.

Now when the icon of the queen disappears, the ceremony reappears, though at a place marked with an absence of ceremony in the sense that the ceremonies that once belonged to this southern land have been forgotten and are no longer performed, though there is Cookalingee dancing out her dance in a theatre which is considered to be the remnants, or the evolution of the old magic circle, the *bora ring* from the Aboriginal centre, or the *amphitheatre* from the European centre. Ceremonies and theatrical performances are magic, that is they are magic-invoking rituals, and so magic is present in my text. The funeral ceremony continues, the bones are crushed and as happens in the Djambidj ceremony, either symbolic or actual, bees begin flying to make their hive in the hollow tree now filled with the pounded bones of the deceased.

It might be appropriate now to talk about some of the icons I have used:

(a) Hollow tree, hollow log signifies a coffin. The bones are interred therein.
(b) Bones: skeletal human bones pounded into pieces.
Reformed to serve as the cells for honey.
(c) Honey: a complex icon. Meanings shift and signifiers disappear into the spiritual. It can signify a strong and potent food, mead, the build-up of a new body different from the old, even the vanished internal organs and flesh. In fact with the honey and the bees, the tree is reincarnated into the living. It more or less takes death away from death, and serves as a symbol of sweet endurance, rejuvenation, rebuilding, rebirth.

Thus with the ceremony, a time of mourning, a time of sadness is rejuvenated into a time of gladness. The funeral ceremony is at the same time an increase ceremony, and is necessary for the continuation of the species . . .

This is shown in the paragraph after the poem and with the vanishing of the drag queen: Cookalingee is seen as the mother of the young man who was killed in the jail cell. It is his funeral service we are witnessing and Cookalingee's dance is also a funeral service and both combine: country and urban, though all this is unseen by the iconic tourists. They see only what they are able to see.

In the last paragraph, the theme of celebration is taken up. The sense of this is that in Aboriginal culture death is an occasion for communities having the same moiety or Dreaming to come together in a ceremony, perform the rituals properly, then conduct any other business. It is a time of retying old ties and strengthening community links. An Aboriginal band, *Warumpi Band*, begins playing at the end of the funeral service. The whole rhythm changes. Mourning becomes celebration; but this is a celebration of increased hope. It is not for an actuality and so the rhythm continues: *shunit, shunit, shunit.* For the celebration is not for the birth of white Australia, but for the survival of the Aborigines over the last two hundred years; of their coming together in Sydney; of the bringing down of ancient ceremonies from the north, and of the laying to rest the corpse of the past. It is a celebration of hope for the future.

Traditional Aboriginal culture is a complexity which does not separate out a literature from ceremony or society. Literature is sung and any prose serves only as a commentary on the songs, though this is changing under the thrust of modernism. Songs are to be sung and experienced in ceremonies or rituals, and the meanings vary to the degree in which a participant has entered into the complete spirituality of the community. Thus signifiers have changing signifieds with the significations depending on the knowledge of the recipient, or the reader. In the new Aboriginal writing—and by new Aboriginal writing I signify writings by such writers as Lionel Fogarty—there has been a shift away from what has been a simple plea, or a writing slanted towards white people. A tool useful for understanding. This early writing did not result in a return of understanding, but in the outrage of critics directed at such writings as being puerile and not as good as European writing. Naturally, this attitude has always been directed at writing which tends towards the straightforwardness of propaganda, and at writing which is meant to be recited publicly, rather than pondered over in the quietness of a person's study.

Aboriginal writing is often meant for public consumption in a public act such as before a crowd of people at a political meeting, and this makes for misunderstanding on the part of those critics who emphasise the aesthetic at the expense of the content, or message. Now, since the works of early Aboriginal writers who emphasised message and accessibility, Aboriginal writing has developed towards a spirituality interested in using and exploring the inner reality of Aboriginality in Australia.

Naturally in doing this there are problems, in that there may be no readership for such a writing, or that those critics who dismissed Aboriginal writing for accessibility may now dismiss it for obscurity. A hope lies in the fact that literary criticism has developed new techniques in working with texts which may appear on the surface obscure. It is refreshing to find that we are far from the dreariness of the conventional: it doesn't rhyme, it doesn't scan, it's not grammatical, it's not poetry, it's not prose, etc. etc.

When the Victorian English critic Matthew Arnold formulated his questions for the book critic, he did not stress conventional grammar and sentence structure as criteria for what is good and what is not, though he most likely accepted this beyond comment. He formulated three questions:

(a) What is the writer trying to do?
(b) How well does he succeed in doing it?
(c) Is it worth doing?

So what is the Aboriginal writer trying to do? Naturally, this varies according to the writer, and many critics and book reviewers still disparage a writer because they don't like what he or she is trying to do, or because he or she is not trying to do something else. This happened when Oodgeroo Noonuccal published her first books and it still continues among some critics and reviewers, though others have come to accept Aboriginal literature as a strong and vibrant Australian literature in its own right.

The second question demands creative reading from the reader. In fact there may not be a definite answer, or you may have to know something of modern critical practice to formulate an answer. One block which occurs here is that the reader when shown how he or she might change his or her reading habits, feels that such an approach destroys the pleasure of reading. Then we must ask what is this *pleasure*, and what are we reading for?

The third question: *Is it worth doing?* Art makes us aware of what we know and don't know that we know. Our conscious awareness, our ego, often seems to support the idea that we know all that we should know, or all that should be known. I see the ego as a master or mistress of illusion, and art and literature might help us to be aware that there is more to the ego than our heads, just as there is more to literature than standard sentences, standard grammar, standard modes of coping with reality.

If it is impossible for us to, for example, change the colour of our skins, or even our sexual preferences, we can come to some understanding of other ways of being by reading about them. And when we begin formulating ideas on exactly why we are reading, why we want to put ourselves in the less than passive position of the reader, we *then* might begin growing and querying some of the things around us.

The act of reading is important, and can be extended beyond books to the many texts surrounding us. Reading is a creative act, and may even extend into that of the creative writer, for after all a creative writer is usually a creative reader, which brings us full circle to the quotation I used at the beginning of this analysis, and now with another reading might render up other meanings:

> . . . that a text is not a line of words releasing a single 'theological' meaning (the 'message' of the Author—God) but a multi-dimensional space in which a variety of writings, none of them original, blend and clash. The text is a tissue of quotations drawn from the innumerable centres of cultures.

Select Bibliography

Aboriginal Access Course. *Aboriginal Student Literature*. Perth: Leederville Technical College, 1984.

Aboriginal Welfare: Initial Conference of Commonwealth and States Aboriginal Authorities, April 1937. Canberra, Government Printer, 1937.

Barthes, Roland. *Image-Music-Text*. Glasgow: Fontana, 1977.

Beckett, Samuel. *Waiting For Godot*. London: Faber and Faber, 1956.

Bennell, Eddie. *Aboriginal Legends from the Bibulmun Tribe*. Adelaide: Rigby, 1981.

Benterrak, K., Muecke, S., & Roe, P. *Reading the Country: Introduction to Nomadology*. Fremantle: Fremantle Arts Press, 1984.

Berndt, C. 'A Drama of North-Eastern Arnhem Land.' *Oceania*, 22 (3), 1952, pp. 216–39.

Berndt, R. M. *Djanggawul*. London: Routledge, 1952.

Berndt, R. M. & C. H. *The World of the First Australians*. Sydney: Ure Smith, 1964.

Boal, Augusto. *Theatre of the Oppressed*. London: Pluto Press, 1979.

Brandenstein, C. G. von & Thomas, A. P. *Taruru: Aboriginal Song Poetry from the Pilbara*. Adelaide: Rigby, 1974.

Bropho, Robert. *Fringedweller*. Chippendale, NSW: Alternative Publishing Cooperative, 1980.

——— 'The Great Journey of the Aboriginal Teenagers', *Limit of Maps*, Spring-Summer, 1985, pp. 19–25.

Clare, M. *Karobran: The Story of an Aboriginal Girl*. Chippendale, NSW: Alternative Publishing Cooperative, 1978.

Chesson, Keith. *Jack Davis, A Life-story*. Melbourne: Dent, 1988.

Chesson, Marlene. 'The Birth, Death and Hopefully Rebirth of the Aboriginal Magazine, *Identity*: Jack Davis talks to Marlene Chesson.' Perth: Murdoch University, School of Human Communication, 1985. Unpublished.

Colbung, Ken. 'Not Land rights, But Land Rites', *Australian Aboriginal Studies*, 2, 1988, pp. 103–110.

Colonial Secretary's Office. Inward correspondence, Letter W2858, Box 171. Melbourne, State Archives.

Coloured Stone. *Konibba Rock*. Alice Springs: Imparja Records, CAAMA, 1984.

―――― *Island of Greed*. Alice Springs: Imparja Records, CAAMA, 1985.

Cook, Albert. *Myth and Language*. Bloomington: Indiana University Press, 1980.

Cornwall, Gareth. 'Evaluating Protest Fiction,' *English In Africa*, 7 (1), March 1980.

Cox, Lucy. *Kimberley Legend*. Perth: Abmusic, n.d.

Davis, Jack. *The First Born*. Sydney: Angus & Robertson, 1970.

―――― *Jagardoo*. Sydney: Methuen, 1978.

―――― *John Pat and Other Poems*. Melbourne: Dent, 1988.

―――― *Kullark and The Dreamers*. Sydney: Currency Press, 1982.

―――― *No Sugar*. Sydney: Currency Press, 1986.

―――― *Barungin*. Sydney: Currency Press, 1989.

Djambidj, An Aboriginal Song Series from Northern Australia. Performed by Frank Gurrmanamana and Frank Malkorda (singers) and Sam Gumugun (didgeridoo). Edited by B. Butler and Stephen Wild. Recording and cassette.

―――― A companion book by M. Clunies Ross & S. Wild. Canberra: AIAS, 1982.

Doobov, Ruth. 'The New Dreamtime: Kath Walker in Australian literature', *Australian Literary Studies*, 6 (1), 1973, pp. 46–55.

Edwards, Jay. 'Structural Analysis of the Afro-American Trickster Tale', *Black Literature & Literary Theory*, edited by H. L. Gates, jun. New York: Methuen, 1984.

Eagleston, R. D., Kaldor, S. & Malcolm, I. B. *English and the Aboriginal Child*. Canberra: Curriculum Development Centre, 1982.

Egan, Ted. *Ted Egan Presents the Kimberley*. Cassette recording produced by the singer, n.d.

Everett, James. *A Black Comedy*. Hobart, 1982. Unpublished drama, ms. with the author.

Fanon, Frantz. *The Wretched of the Earth*. Harmondsworth: Penguin Books, 1973.

Fogarty, Lionel. *Jagera*. Coominya: C. Buchanan, 1989 (?).

―――― *Kargun*. Coominya: C. Buchanan, 1980.

―――― *Kudjela*. Coominya: C. Buchanan, 1983.

―――― *Ngutji*. Brisbane: C. Buchanan, 1984.

―――― *Yoogum Yoogum*. Ringwood: Penguin Books, 1982.

Gale, Fay, editor. *We Are Bosses Ourselves*. Canberra: AIAS, 1983.

Gelber, Jack. *The Apple*. New York: Grove Press, 1960.

Gilbert, Kevin J. *Because a White Man'll Never Do It*. Sydney: Angus & Robertson, 1973.

―――― 'Black Policies', *Aboriginal Writing Today*, edited by J. Davis & B. Hodge. Canberra: AIAS, 1985. pp. 35–41.

_____ *The Cherry Pickers*. Canberra: Burrambinga Books, 1988.

_____ *Living Black: Blacks Talk to Kevin Gilbert*. Ringwood: Penguin Books, 1984.

_____ *Inside Black Australia, an Anthology of Aboriginal Poetry*. Ringwood: Penguin Books, 1988.

_____ *People Are Legends: Aboriginal Poems*. St. Lucia: University of Queensland Press, 1978.

Grotowski, Jerzy. *Towards a Poor Man's Theatre*. Wolstebro, Denmark: Odin Teatrets Forlag, 1968.

Halliday, M. A. K. *Language As A Social Semiotic. The Social Interpretation of Language and Meaning*. London: Edward Arnold, 1978.

Hall, Rodney, editor. *The Collins Book of Australian Poetry*. Sydney: Collins, 1981.

Hercus, Luise A. 'The Languages of Victoria: A Late Survey.' *Australian Aboriginal Studies* 17. Canberra: AIAS, 1969.

Identity (Aboriginal and Islander Identity). Sydney, Perth, Canberra, Aboriginal Publications Foundation, 1972–1982.

Keneally, Thomas. *The Chant of Jimmy Blacksmith*. Sydney: Angus & Robertson, 1972.

Keogh, Ray. 'Nurlu Songs from West Kimberley: An Introduction', *Australian Aboriginal Studies* 1, 1989, pp. 2–11.

Kuckles. *Brand New Day (Milliya Rumurra)*. Broome: Mamabulanjin Resource Centre, n.d.

Langford, Ruby. *Don't Take Your Love To Town*. Ringwood: Penguin Books, 1988.

Laughton, Herbie. *Herbie Laughton*. Alice Springs: Imparja-CAAMA, n.d.

Lewis, Oscar. *La Vida*. New York: Random House, 1965.

Lockwood, Douglas. *I, the Aboriginal*. Adelaide: Rigby, 1962.

McDonald, G. *Red Over Black*. Bullsbrook: Veritas, 1984.

McGuinness, Bruce & Walker, Denis. 'The Politics of Aboriginal Literature', *Aboriginal Writing Today*, edited by J. Davis & B. Hodge. Canberra: AIAS, 1985, pp. 43–54.

Mandelbaum, Davis G. 'The Study of Life History: Gandhi', *Current Anthropology*, 14 (3), June 1973, pp. 177–196.

Maris, H. & Borg, S. *Women of the Sun*. Video text. Sydney: Currency Press, 1983.

_____ *Women of the Sun*. Ringwood: Penguin Books, 1985.

Mattingley, C. & Hampton, K. *Survival In Our Own Land. 'Aboriginal' Experiences in 'South Australia' since 1886*. Told by Nungas and others. Adelaide: Wakefield Press, 1988.

Meanjin. Aboriginal Issue, 36 (4), 1977.

Memmi, Albert. *The Colonizer and the Colonized*. London: Souvenir Press, 1974.

Merritt, Robert J. *The Cake Man*. Sydney: Currency Press, 1978.

_____ 'Eora Corroboree', (video text), *Impact*, ABC, Channel 2, screened 13 September 1986.

Miller, James. *Koori: A Will to Win*. Sydney: Angus & Robertson, 1985.

Morgan, Sally. *My Place*. Fremantle: Fremantle Arts Centre Press, 1987.

Mulvaney, D. J. 'The Australian Aborigines 1606–1929: Opinion and Fieldwork, Part 1: 1606–1859', *Historical Studies, Australian and New Zealand*, 8 (30), May 1958.

Murray, Les. *The New Oxford Book of Australian Verse*. Melbourne: Oxford University Press, 1986.

Mutiso, G-C. M. *Socio-political Thought in African Literature*. London: Macmillan, 1974.

Nangan, Joe. *Joe Nangan's Dreaming, Aboriginal Legends of the North-West*. Melbourne: Nelson, 1976.

Narogin, Mudrooroo. *Dalwurra*. Perth: Centre for Studies in Australian Literature, 1988.

—— *Doin Wildcat*. Melbourne, Hyland House, 1988.

—— *Dr Wooreddy's Prescription for Enduring The Ending of the World*. Melbourne: Hyland House, 1983.

—— 'Guerilla poetry: Lionel Fogarty's Response to Language Genocide', *Westerly*, 3, 1986, pp. 47–55.

—— *Long Live Sandawara*. Melbourne: Quartet Books, 1979. Paperback, Melbourne: Hyland House, 1987.

—— 'Reading the Book', review of *Reading the Country*, *Australian Journal of Cultural Studies*, Dec. 1985, 3 (2), pp. 143–146.

—— *The Song Circle of Jacky and Selected Poems*. Melbourne: Hyland House, 1986.

—— 'The Writer as "Bricoleur"; the Novel as "Bricolage", Yambo Ouoluguem and *Le Devoir de Violence*'. Unpublished paper, 1985.

—— *Wildcat Falling*. Sydney: Angus & Robertson, 1965.

No Fixed Address. *From My Eyes*. Melbourne: Rough Diamond Records, 1982.

—— *Wrong Side of the Road*. Adelaide: Black Australian Records (EMI), 1981.

Noonuccal, Oodgeroo (Walker, Kath). *The Dawn Is At Hand*. Brisbane: Jacaranda, 1966.

—— *My People*. Brisbane: Jacaranda, 1970.

—— *We Are Going*. Brisbane: Jacaranda, 1964.

Ouologuem, Yambo. *Bound to Violence*. London: Secker & Warburg, 1968.

Perkins, Charles. *A Bastard Like Me*. Sydney: Ure Smith, 1975.

Polanyi, Livia. 'Telling the Same Story Twice', *Text*, 1 (4), 1981, pp. 315–336.

Randall, Bob, *Bob Randall*. Alice Springs: Imparja-CAAMA records, n.d.

Rasmussen, Dennis. *Poetry and Truth*. The Hague: Mouton, 1975.

Reynolds, Henry, editor. *Aborigines and Settlers: The Australian Experience 1788–1839*. Sydney: Cassell, 1972.

Riffaterre, Michael. *Semiotics of Poetry*. London: Methuen, 1980.

Roe, Paddy. *Gularabulu*, edited by S. Muecke. Fremantle: Fremantle Arts Press, 1983.

Rosenblatt, Roger. 'Black Autobiography: Life as a Death Weapon', *Autobiography: Essays Theoretical and Critical*, edited by J. Olney. Princeton: Princeton University Press, 1980.

Roughsey, Elsie (Labumore). *An Aboriginal Mother Tells of the Old and the New*. Fitzroy: McPhee Gribble, 1984.

Schules, Robert. *Semiotics and Interpretation*. New Haven: Yale University Press, 1982.

Shaw, Bruce. *Banggaiyerri, the Story of Jack Sullivan As Told To Bruce Shaw*. Canberra: AIAS, 1983.

_____ *My Country of the Pelican Dreaming. The Life of an Australian Aborigine of the Gadjerong, Grant Ngabidj, 1904–1977 As Told To Bruce Shaw*. Canberra: AIAS, 1981.

Shoemaker, Adam. 'Aboriginal Creative Writing: A Survey to 1981', *Aboriginal History*, 6 (2), 1982, pp. 111–129.

_____ 'Drama In Black and White — Race Relations Theatre in Australia since 1970'. Typescript, 1981.

_____ *Black Words White Page, Aboriginal Literature 1929–1988*. St. Lucia: University of Queensland Press, 1989.

Simon, Ella. *Through My Eyes*. Adelaide: Rigby, 1978. Second edition, Blackburn: Collins Dove, 1987.

Skipper, Peter. *The Pushman*. Fitzroy Crossing: SIL, 198-?

Strehlow, T. G. H. *Songs of Central Australia*. Sydney: Angus & Robertson, 1971.

Sullivan, C. 'Non-Tribal Dance Music and Song, From First Contact To Citizen Rights', *Australian Aboriginal Studies* 1, 1988, pp. 64–67.

Summer Institute of Linguistics. *Work Papers of SIL-AAB, series b. Vols. 3, 4 & 5*. Darwin: SIL, 1979–82.

Sykes, Bobbi. *Love Poems and other Revolutionary Actions*. Cammaray: Saturday Centre, 1979.

Tatz, Colin. *Black Viewpoints*. Sydney: Angus & Robertson, 1975.

Taylor, Andrew. Review of *The Dawn Is At Hand*, by Kath Walker, *Overland*, 36, May 1967, p. 44.

Thomas, William. *Papers, set 214, Uncatalogued MSS*. Sydney, Mitchell Library.

Tunstill, Guy. 'An Overview of the Centre for Aboriginal Studies in Music 1988, *Australian Aboriginal Studies* 1, 1989, pp. 29–30.

Us Mob. *Wrong Side of the Road*. Adelaide: Black Australian Records (EMI), 1981.

Ward, Glenyse. *Wandering Girl*. Broome: Magabala Books, 1988.

Walker, Denis (with McGuinness, B.). 'The Politics of Aboriginal Literature', *Aboriginal Writing Today*, edited by J. Davis & B. Hodge. Canberra: AIAS, 1985, pp. 43–54.

Wellek, R. & Warren, A. *Theory of Literature*. Harmondsworth: Penguin Books, 1973.

Watego, Cliff, 'Aboriginal Poetry and White Criticism', *Aboriginal Writing Today*, edited by J. Davis & B. Hodge. Canberra: AIAS, 1985, pp. 75–90.

Webb, Hugh. 'Conning Popular Music: Up Against the Wall', *Australian Journal of Cultural Studies*, 21, 1984, pp. 99–109.

―――― 'The Reggae-Folk Protest: Australian Pop Music and Ideology', *Literature and Popular Culture*, edited by H. Ruthrof and J. Fiske. *Australian Journal of Cultural Studies* (Special Issue).

Weller, Archie. *The Day of the Dog*. Sydney: Pan Books, 1981.

―――― *Going Home*. Sydney: Allen & Unwin, 1986.

Wendt, Albert. *Leaves of the Banyan Tree*. Harmondsworth: Penguin Books, 1981.

Willmot, Eric. *Pemulwuy, The Rainbow Warrior*. McMahons Point: Weldon, 1987.

Index